COAST GUARD
MIRACLES OF NEW ORLEANS

COAST GUARD
MIRACLES OF NEW ORLEANS

CAPT ROBERT MUELLER, USCG (ret)

**Foreword by Rear Adm. Joseph Castillo,
U.S. Coast Guard (ret)**

PELICAN PUBLISHING
NEW ORLEANS

First published by Pelican Publishing Company, Inc. as
Coast Guard Heroes of New Orleans, 2016
First Pelican Publishing printing, 2023

ISBN 9781455626960
Ebook ISBN 9781455626977

Printed in the United States of America

Published by Pelican Publishing
New Orleans, LA
www.pelicanpub.com

Contents

"I have called you back from the ends of the earth so you can serve me. For I have chosen you and will not throw you away. Don't be afraid, for I am with you. Do not be dismayed, for I am your God. I will strengthen you. I will help you. I will uphold you with my victorious right hand."

Isaiah 41: 9-10

And so it was with the Coast Guard in
New Orleans, in September of 2005.

Foreword

Hurricane Katrina in New Orleans (or just plain "Katrina" to those who went through it) was one of the most horrible things to ever happen in United States history. General William Tecumseh Sherman said in 1864, "War is hell," and for those who were there for the hurricane and the immediate aftermath in New Orleans, Katrina was its own hell. This is not to diminish the fact that the devastation was not exclusively New Orleans'. Mississippi suffered terrible coastal damage, and the Gulf Coast all the way to western Mobile, Alabama, was hit as well. But New Orleans is a bowl—the lowest land in the area, with levees circling it to protect it from the water that surrounds it, with little to no natural drainage—and that bowl flooded. And it remained flooded for weeks with sewage and chemicals and water-filled cars and debris and uprooted animals—and people.

The news media did a pretty good job of depicting much of the hell. However, until 360-degree, total-immersion television complete with "smell-vision" comes along, the viewing audience can still look up from the TV scene of utter devastation and deprivation and see the nicely framed pictures of their parents and close friends and glance outside to take in the green grass through their window. Then they can drive to a nearby store to pick up the rolls they forgot for their turkey dinner, without having to wade through three feet of water and muck and floating mayhem in their house and reach the driveway only to discover their car has floated away. If you weren't there, you simply cannot understand the horror.

Some people took advantage of the situation to act out their fantasies or personalities of violence and anarchy and chaos. And the media did a great job of recording and presenting those visual or written images to the United States and the world too. But the media stories missed a lot.

How do I know? I was the Eighth District Chief of Operations and the Forward Chief of Staff to Rear Admiral Bob Duncan, who was the District Commander and in charge of the overall rescue and response operations, which rescued or evacuated well over 33,500 people. My shipmates—and good friends— Captains Frank Paskewich and Bob Mueller were the Sector New Orleans Commander and Deputy Commander, respectively, and worked for Admiral Duncan. They ran the marine safety, port security, waterborne search and rescue side of things, while Captain Bruce Jones ran the air side of search and rescue. These three men have my greatest respect for their efforts, and I'd work disasters with any of them again in a heartbeat.

I'll grant you that the event was so huge that no one person could know everything that went on. This, too, I know because I was there. I was there from the moment Katrina weakened to tropical storm force winds until I was transferred a year later, flying into the city virtually every day and then based in the city in a rented RV from day ten until I was needed elsewhere and promoted to a job in Cleveland, Ohio, a year later. Resources flowed in from all over the country, and nearly one-quarter of the Coast Guard force was there at one point or another. And despite being there, I don't know everything that happened. Whenever some of us survivors get together—after the obligatory and universal "How'd you make out?"—I learn another piece of the story. And yet, it's clear to me that the media stories that came out unduly focused on the negative.

There's plenty of negative to be sure, but also plenty of positive. While Katrina brought out the worst in many, it also brought out the best in many. And that best was not recorded and presented to the world as well, or as frequently, as the rest.

Take the Kenner policeman who lost his home, lost his dog, and didn't know where his family was. But when citizens were briefly allowed back into the city (for only one day) to gather essential items from their homes a week after Katrina, he was driving the neighborhoods with tears in his eyes, bringing bottles of water and whatever assistance he could provide.

Or the doctor whose office was in Metairie, where a Coast Guard boat crew found themselves throttling a story or two above the flooded street. Desperately short on medical supplies from treating wounded and injured, they broke the upper-story window and went in to gather first-aid supplies and equipment. The doctor was contacted after things got back to "normal" and given a list of the items taken and a claim form to recover the damages. He wrote a very nice note back commending the boat crew for doing the right thing and returning the claim form, saying to consider the items his donation to the cause.

Some of the strength of the Coast Guard response came from our motto of *"Semper Paratus,"* Always Ready. Much came from our focus on "trained initiative" and insisting on decision-making at the lowest levels. But even more came from our standardized training, which allows a pilot from Houston, a co-pilot from Miami, a flight mechanic from Los Angeles, and a rescue swimmer from Detroit to meet each other at the aircraft for the first time, shake hands, and fly into some of the most dangerous conditions any of them have ever experienced, taking their machines and personal skills to the limit. In high heat and humidity, overloaded with people and lifesaving supplies, threading rescue swimmers between trees or downed power lines and gas-fueled fires, they drew strength from each other, each trusting the other to have been trained exactly the same way, to have all the equipment stowed on the helicopter in exactly the same place, and to know that each of them have a place in the long blue line where others before them have performed to the limits of their ability and others behind them will look at their performance and draw inspiration from it in their own time of testing.

We drew strength as well from the Coasties who came from around the country to help. Almost half our aircraft and probably over a quarter of our entire force came at some point to help support the effort. I was always left with a sense of pride and inspiration whenever I was at a gathering of our people and I saw a sea of ball caps with different unit names embroidered on the front. That was such a simple and visible sign of our solidarity with each other—and an instant opening with somebody you didn't personally know: "Hey, I used to be stationed there!" Unfortunately, years later a change to the uniform regulations removed the embroidered unit names, leaving only "U.S. Coast Guard." Its attempt to increase uniformity took away part of what brought us together at disaster sites.

Missing in the public narrative are stories such as these. Stories of solidarity, friendship, and community, of neighborhoods coming together to help each other rebuild with brick and mortar as well as emotionally and mentally. Gang stories are easy to find, but not so much the stories of love for fellow man.

This book helps to fill that void, with a little different focus. Its focus is on positive things that don't seem possible without divine intervention. Sometimes that intervention set things in motion years earlier, to allow someone to have the skill set needed for those fateful days. Captain Bob Mueller was one of those people with an unusual career path, having Joint Forces, Navy, and NATO experience, not exactly standard career building blocks for a boat forces officer. Throw in an assignment with base operations in Puerto Rico, where he turned the unit's boats into a full-fledged search and rescue, law enforcement, multi-mission station; add in some intelligence and operations planning work; and finish it off with a previous assignment in Mobile, Alabama, and you end up with the right person to be in the city leading the dedicated, innovative, and hard-charging young Coast Guard men and women we were all privileged to serve with and call shipmates.

If you don't live a faith-based life, read this book to discover some of the incredible events that transpired during the course of the Katrina rescue and recovery but weren't published by the papers, magazines, TV, and radio shows. You will walk away with a better understanding—a more complete picture—of what happened during Katrina. If you do live a faith-based life, you will see God's hand at work, and you will walk away inspired by how people accomplish his purpose in this world.

Rear Admiral Joseph "Pepe" Castillo
U.S. Coast Guard (retired)
Chesapeake, Virginia
April 2016

Introduction

It was a sunny, late spring day in Virginia, a really beautiful day that enduring a winter of record snow makes you appreciate even more. But despite the warm blue skies, things in my heart were stormy.

It was transfer season, and I was wondering where the Coast Guard was going to send me for my next assignment. I had just been promoted to captain the year before, but it wasn't a good year for Operations Ashore guys like me, the officers running the system of rescue and law enforcement stations all along the U.S. coast.

Typically some years have more openings than others, and 2005 didn't have many openings at all. I had made my request for the assignments I wanted, and I thought I had a little pull. So when the call came from the assignment officer on that bright and sunny day, I was a bit surprised when he said New Orleans.

And in the United States Coast Guard they don't give out invitations; they issue orders. So New Orleans it was.

I didn't know much about New Orleans, but it wasn't a big search and rescue area like other areas in the Coast Guard, and SAR was what I wanted to get back to after two years in a staff assignment. Along with search and rescue, my career had included assignments with the Navy and Joint Operations and even a short NATO tour in Italy working the Bosnian war with our European allies. I had an unusual background for a Coast Guard officer and given that, an assignment in New Orleans, where marine safety was the primary Coast Guard mission, really didn't make much sense to me. I remember saying, "I don't know what is going to happen in New Orleans, but God wants me there for some reason."

I had no way of knowing that within a few months I would be leading the largest surface search and rescue operation in U.S. Coast Guard history to save more than twenty-five thousand people from the flooded city of New Orleans in the aftermath of the deadly Hurricane Katrina. I would be using every bit of my Joint Forces experience to work with the Navy, Army, Marines, National Guard, and local law enforcement, as well as nearly every federal agency in existence. Come the end of August 2005, I would see ordinary people do extraordinary things. I would see the very worst in humanity, but also the very best we have to offer. And I would see miracles, situations where there was no explanation other than that the Lord was involved.

I will share the stories of those ordinary people who became heroes during Hurricane Katrina. There are many stories of that time, both good and bad. The bad stories received plenty of air time during the storm period, but few have heard of the amazing things that happened. I can only write about what I was involved with and know to be true. Sadly, there will be many stories left untold, many heroes unreported, and with a disaster and rescue operation of this magnitude, that is regrettably unavoidable.

But this is what I saw before, during, and immediately after Hurricane Katrina. These are stories that need to be told.

The One-Armed Bandit

Katrina slammed United States Coast Guard Station New Orleans that Monday morning, August 28, 2005, the water rushing in from Lake Pontchartrain, submerging the boat slips and flooding everything under the station building. Massive amounts of water relentlessly roiled under the building, destroying the boat repair shop with its critical tools and parts, and turning the private vehicles of the crew into miniature submarines. Everything was consumed by fifteen feet of water. The old wooden restaurants out over the lake, local icons, were rapidly dismantled by the wind and their shredded remains blown toward the station. The massive flood washed the debris into, under, and around the station, and then it overtopped the levee. The Bucktown neighborhood directly behind the station and the Lakeview neighborhood to the east were in grave danger from the water surging into the 17th Street Canal that ran between the neighborhoods. And the water in that canal was rising fast.

Fortunately for Bucktown, the water did not overtop the lake levee for very long, and though the smaller I-wall levee that ran alongside their side of the 17th Street Canal bent and twisted, it did not break, at least not on the Bucktown side. The adjacent Lakeview neighborhood was not so lucky. The levee on their side of the 17th Street Canal breeched, instantly inundating the neighborhood and its homes with water twenty feet deep in some spots. Some residents close to the break later said they had about thirty seconds to get into their attics as the water chased them up the stairs. Once marooned in the attic with whatever they happened to have in their hands at the time, they waited in total darkness as their former homes were engulfed by a brown, brackish sea. This disaster in the Lakeview neighborhood transpired about 150 yards from Station New Orleans and what would become the center of the Katrina rescue operation.

Station New Orleans is a small boat rescue station on Lake Pontchartrain, built near the Bucktown and Lakeview neighborhoods in New Orleans and next to the 17th Street Canal, which separates the two communities. Significantly the station was built outside the lake levee, right on the shore of the huge lake itself. The entire building was built on concrete pilings and was designed to withstand Category 4 hurricane winds and the likely flooding that would result from such a storm. The idea was that the water could wash in underneath the building and then drain out again, and that is exactly what happened during the storm.

The building served as a combined Group headquarters on one side and a small boat station on the other. The station side held a few offices and an operations center manned by "Coasties" twenty-four hours a day. The operations center responded to urgent radio traffic and phone calls and launched rescue boats or helicopters as needed for various rescue or emergency situations. The station side of the building held living spaces for the boat crews, a galley for food preparation and dining, and offices for the station staff, as well as room for boat and engine repair on the ground floor. The Group headquarters was staffed by senior officers who supervised four rescue stations: Station Gulfport, Station Venice, Station Grand Isle, and, of course, Station New Orleans.

But the Coast Guard was changing, and in the summer of 2005, the rescuc-focused groups were being combined with the industry-focused Marine Safety Office to form a new headquarters called a "Sector." The old Group New Orleans was located at the station on Lake Pontchartrain, while the old Marine Safety Office New Orleans was located downtown. The new combined Sector headquarters were to take over the old Group headquarters and its operations center, with much of the staff being located in downtown New Orleans at the old Marine Safety Office location. During the weeks leading up to Katrina and for three years after, the newly renamed Sector/Station New Orleans served as the headquarters for Sector New Orleans, with about sixty people working in the former Group offices designed for only twenty. Despite the reorganization, the station remained a rescue station to support about four or five rescue boats and the crews that manned them. The rest of the Sector staff, more than one hundred people, worked in downtown New Orleans across from the Superdome.

As Katrina approached that last weekend in August, Coast Guard personnel followed the routine procedures in place in the face of any threatened hurricane. Standard policy called for the station to evacuate equipment and people before the storm and prepare to return fully operational as soon as possible in its wake. For the Sector headquarters personnel, that meant evacuation to Alexandria, Louisiana, about four hours away, to set up a command center capable of overseeing disaster recovery. For Station New Orleans, with its boats and people focused on search and rescue, that meant making sure the boats were safe from the storm and then ready to launch.

The station's Commanding Officer, Chief Warrant Officer Dan Brooks, had to trailer his smaller boats to safe locations on the north shore of Lake Pontchartrain, beyond the possible reach of any floodwaters. He also had to get his larger 41-foot utility boats underway to safety. They would travel with 41-footers from other rescue stations and the larger aid to navigation boats, all evacuating up the Mississippi River to the north of Baton Rouge with a Coast Guard river tender to serve as mother ship for the boats. Their destination would hopefully take them out of the way of the storm. His crews left their cars at the station, nobody really expecting the flooding that came.

Frankly, nobody expected anything like what was to come. Most Coasties anticipated they would be gone for two or three days—as with every other major hurricane "scare" for the past forty years—and packed accordingly. They followed procedure: prepare, get the boats out, secure the station, be ready for anything. Yet they thought they would return to business as usual within a few days. Chief Warrant Officer Brooks had done a fine job preparing his command for the storm. His boats were safe, his crews were well trained, properly evacuated and ready, and his station building was locked down and secure, the windows shuttered and closed up tight. But no one could have prepared for what would hit New Orleans that Monday morning.

Lake Pontchartrain, on the north side of New Orleans, is twenty-four miles wide, and while only about ten to fourteen feet deep in most parts, it holds a significant amount of water. But during Katrina it probably held at least twice its normal volume. As the storm built into the monster it became, it pushed the salty waters of the Gulf of Mexico ahead of it, producing an overwhelming storm surge. Katrina in New Orleans was mostly a water event, with the storm surge doing most of the devastation. As the winds of Katrina built stronger and stronger, it pushed more and more water ahead of it. Katrina not only reached Category 5 on the wind scale, but it was truly a massive storm, reaching from Texas to Florida, with significant flooding as far east as Mobile, Alabama. As Katrina headed for New Orleans and grew in size, its counter-clockwise winds forced the water north and then west as the winds circulated around the eye of the storm.

Look at a map of the Gulf Coast, and you will see that the lower part of Louisiana, centered on the Mississippi River, is much farther south than the coast of Mississippi. An inlet to Lake Pontchartrain is nestled north of the mouth of the river. The geography of the Louisiana and Mississippi coastlines acted like a funnel for the massive surge Katrina was building and forced the water into the shallow lake. The wall of water annihilated the elevated Interstate 10 over the eastern edge of the lake, washing its concrete structures away like they were made of soft mud. The lake rose higher and higher, with a fifteen-foot rush of water flooding the northern shores of the lake into the cities of Slidell and Mandeville, destroying homes and businesses and washing away anything in its path. And the lake rose higher still, flooding farther north and west to Madisonville and washing away the massive concrete turn-arounds of the Southbound span of the Causeway Bridge connecting the north and south shores of the lake, and then as the storm passed north of New Orleans, the winds turned south and forced all this water into New Orleans, aimed directly at the Bucktown and Lakeview neighborhoods.

The small levees on either side of the 17th Street Canal had been designed to make sure water flowed out of New Orleans and into the lake, and, to be sure, they could hold back water from Lake Pontchartrain in case of a flood. But this flood was beyond anything they could hope to withstand. As the storm passed to the northeast of New Orleans, all that water that was shoved into Lake Pontchartrain was now being blown south at a rapid rate, and the lake's levels began to rise dramatically. As the water flooded Station New Orleans and rose all along the large and very strong earthen lake levee, it was also rapidly rising against the smaller canal I-wall levees on both sides of the canal. The I-wall levees are so named because in cross-section, they resemble the capital letter I. On both sides of the canal, these reinforced concrete levee walls were straining and starting to buckle, but the water kept rising and rising. Foundations were being stressed and starting to give way on both sides, and still the water kept rising.

This is what Mike Howell faced that Monday morning when Katrina hit. He was living onboard his converted fishing boat *Mañana*. The *Mañana* was a fifty-five-foot steel boat Mike had turned into his floating home. He purchased the boat in the mid-1970s, installed a running engine and significantly modified below decks, creating nice living quarters, including

Mike Howell, the "One Armed Bandit." (USCG, Mike Howell)

Mañana *at Coast Guard Station New Orleans. (USCG, Mike Howell)*

a galley for cooking and a shower. Mike then earned his commercial captain's license from the Coast Guard and made a living with *Mañana* working in the Gulf of Mexico. Mike lived aboard *Mañana* for years with his beloved dogs, and he was always a cheerful face willing to help.

And Mike was aboard *Mañana* in the harbor of the New Orleans Yacht Club when Katrina came calling. Sunday night, as the winds gained strength with the storm's approach, howling through the masts and wires of the boats in the harbor, *Mañana* softly bounced up and down with the increasing waves. By early morning the wind was screaming over 120 miles per hour, ripping shingles and roofs apart, uprooting trees, and tossing fiberglass yachts about like toys. But *Mañana,* built of heavy steel, remained where she belonged, in the water. That water was rising quickly and Mike rapidly worked his lines to keep his home safe. Other boats in the marina were sunk or otherwise totally destroyed by the rapidly rising water, docks were tossed and twisted, buildings ashore were washed away. Yet through it all, Mike and *Mañana* bumped and banged along. Mike had lost an arm in Vietnam, where he served in the Army as a door gunner in combat helicopters, one of the more dangerous jobs in that war. Working quickly with his one good arm and using his plastic arm as a brace, he worked his lines in the face of the storm, fended off debris, including other boats, and comforted his dogs, who were frantic with fear.

When the storm had passed, Mike looked around to a world of total destruction. Nothing was as it should be. Buildings were gone and boats were scattered about like toys, some tossed on top of others. Mike set about getting *Mañana* squared away and helping others where he could.

He was no stranger to hard times; in Vietnam his arm was shattered by bullets, he was shot through the leg, and his body was peppered with shrapnel. The doctors expected him to die, but he refused, and in retrospect, the Lord obviously had other plans for him. In 1980, when 125,000 people were

Mike's view from Mañana *in the harbor of the New Orleans Yacht Club as Katrina passed over the city. (USCG, Mike Howell)*

fleeing Cuba during the Mariel Boatlift, Mike set out from New Orleans on *Mañana* and rescued 75 people, mostly women and children. One sixteen-year-old girl he rescued later wrote a book called *Finding Mañana* and won the Pulitzer Prize for her story. Nobody told Mike to go to Cuba; he just thought he should help.

Along with being a decorated combat veteran, Mike Howell was also a dedicated Coast Guard Auxiliarist. The Auxiliary is a volunteer branch. They are dedicated men and women who give their time and effort to the Coast Guard and often use their vessels and aircraft for the Coast Guard mission. The Auxiliary is very important to the Coast Guard, and in Katrina they were essential to the entire operation's success. While these volunteers cannot undertake law enforcement or foul weather search and rescue, they engage in overflights, help with training practice for regular Coast Guard members and teams, provide local knowledge, conduct safety inspections of vessels, and perform a host of other important missions vital to the Coast Guard. Mike was a great Auxiliarist, always willing to help with whatever needed to be done. He participated in many search and rescue operations and let Coast Guard boarding teams hone their skills while conducting training boardings of *Mañana*. So after the storm had passed and his vessel was ready, Mike took *Mañana* to the nearby Coast Guard Station New Orleans. Without a doubt, *Mañana* was the only vessel underway on the lake that day.

But the station Mike found after the storm was not the squared-away military base he knew and loved. The white

Yachts were tossed ashore by Katrina's storm surge. Other vessels were sunk or completely destroyed. Mike safely rode out the storm aboard Mañana *and then set out for Coast Guard Station New Orleans. (USCG, Mike Howell)*

Coast Guard Station New Orleans, with the wreckage of restaurants piled on the levee behind it. (USCG, Mike Howell)

building on pilings still stood proud, its red tile roof and green shutters largely intact, but the remains of the wooden restaurants that formerly lined the nearby lakefront were piled everywhere, along with everything from inside the restaurants: walls, tables, chairs, plates, roofs, equipment, pots, pans, everything. The critical small boat repair workshops under the building were destroyed, and cars parked under the building when the crews left were ruined. A small fire shot forth from the ground, a cracked gas line that would remain ablaze for weeks. The docks were covered with debris, and Mike set to work on making them serviceable for the Coast Guard men and women whom he knew would soon return.

It must have seemed surreal to Mike to have Station New Orleans all to himself. The surrounding neighborhoods, like much of New Orleans and its suburbs, were also empty.

Most of the residents of both Bucktown and Lakeview had evacuated before the storm arrived, many on Saturday and more on Sunday. New Orleans had seen more than its share of hurricanes and false alarms over the years, and for many people, Hurricane Betsy in 1965, when New Orleans last flooded, was but a distant memory. And they had faith in the levees, much higher and stronger now than they had been during Betsy. Technology, too, was much better. Surely they were safe from any storm.

Yet Katrina was different. It was so much bigger and stronger than any other hurricane had been. On Friday night the storm had suddenly changed direction and seemed to be headed straight for New Orleans. Everybody was talking about evacuating. The local governments of the parishes south of the lake warned people on Saturday to evacuate, but people in the greater New Orleans area sometimes don't pay much attention to what the government might or might not say. However, they do watch the Weather Channel, a local tradition during hurricane season, and when Jim Cantori said he was coming to New Orleans to report on the storm, people took notice. We all love Jim, but when he says he's coming to your city during hurricane season, it's never good news. People all over the New Orleans area burned up the phone lines talking with relatives and friends, exchanging opinions and discussing options. Most reached the same conclusion: it was time to leave.

It was without a doubt the most orderly and effective evacuation of a major city in modern history. With most hurricanes you have five or six days' warning, but on Friday morning Katrina seemed to be headed for the Florida panhandle, and it was only on Friday evening that it became clear that the massive storm was headed for New Orleans with expected landfall Monday morning, only two and a half days away. However, even with this very compressed timeline, barely sixty hours, the evacuation unfolded with amazing smoothness. Exact numbers will never be known, but New Orleans and nearby Jefferson Parish turned into huge ghost towns overnight as an estimated eighty-five to ninety percent of the population headed north, east, and west. With over half a million people in New Orleans proper alone, that means more than 440,000 people evacuated, and probably close to that number left nearby Jefferson Parish as well. In low-lying St. Bernard and Plaquemines Parishes, farther south of New Orleans, nearly every person who could possibly leave did so. These figures are astounding. After the fact, many talking heads on television and government officials who should have known better criticized the people of New Orleans for not leaving before the storm. But this shows a complete disregard for the facts. New Orleans did evacuate. For the first time in modern history a major U.S. city emptied itself in two days, smoothly, efficiently, and without riot or fanfare.

But not everybody could or would leave. Some of the less fortunate couldn't afford to leave, and others simply didn't have a place to go. Some of the older residents weren't as mobile as they had been when they were younger, and the trip seemed too difficult. And some were worried about their pets. Common knowledge was that hotels in general wouldn't allow animals, so some stayed because they wouldn't leave behind their beloved dogs and cats. Finally, like every major city, New Orleans had its criminal element, and many of those remained behind as well.

For the few residents remaining in the Bucktown and Lakeview neighborhoods, mostly middle and upper-middle class, time was running out. The water was now rising very quickly in the 17th Street Canal, and the I-wall levees on both sides were buckling, rapidly giving way. The Lakeview side failed first. The initial breach was very small, but it rapidly expanded until the water poured through, ripping the levee apart on that side as billions of gallons hemorrhaged forth. Those few people remaining in houses near the Lakeview breach rushed to the attic, where a very few had left an axe up there just in case a Betsy-type flood ever came again and they needed to chop their way out. Most had nothing except the junk we all have in our attics, which unfortunately doesn't include food, water, or tools. For those survivors in Lakeview, their homes now under as much as twenty feet of water, life changed in an instant.

Some survived in the flooded neighborhoods, and some of those survivors made their way to Station New Orleans, standing bright white and clearly intact, just on the other side of the massive levee on the lake. Some were just scared and hungry; some were bruised and battered from the storm; one lady was quite pregnant; and others had criminal intent. The latter broke into the building through heavily secured doors. Once inside, they proceeded to loot and destroy everything. Eventually sixty-three people invaded the station building, stealing clothes from the bunk rooms, taking food and anything they could carry, urinating on the beds, and smearing feces on the walls. They rendered much of the station building uninhabitable until it could be sterilized, which wouldn't be for some time.

Mike saw some of this from *Mañana,* but there wasn't much he could do, so he tended to his boat and his dogs, and he worked to make things better on the docks. And as he knew they would, the Coasties did come back.

On the north shore of the lake, CWO Brooks was working to get his boats and crews to the lake, but they were facing their own gauntlet. The boat crews had sheltered well inland from the lake to protect the boats, and now they had to chop through downed trees to clear the roads. And downed trees were everywhere on what had been the heavily wooded north shore. They cleared their way to the Maritime Museum in Madisonville, which had a good boat ramp from which they could launch. But people in Madisonville, and indeed all along the north shore of Lake Pontchartrain, were in trouble as well, and the Coasties found themselves helping scores of people along the way. Eventually the Coasties hacked their way to the water, launched their boats, and seven brave men and women got their boats underway for New Orleans, with no idea what lay ahead for them.

Boatswain's Mate Second Class Jessica Guidroz was the boat coxswain for one of the small boats headed back to the station. As coxswain, she was in charge of the boat. In her early twenties, Petty Officer Guidroz was a veteran of many Coast Guard missions, and she was not only well trained, she was ready. When they arrived at the station, the young crew were shocked at what they found. As they entered the station building, some of the survivors were happy to see them, to see law and order return. But the criminals were not impressed. Jessica Guidroz and her crew were in no mood to tolerate any nonsense, and the seven Coasties quickly rounded up the sixty-three intruders. Along with being highly trained for rescue operations, the Station New Orleans boat crews are highly trained law enforcement officers. Once the unsavory people were in custody, the Coasties confiscated 15 knives, 2 handguns, a claw hammer, 5 bags of marijuana, a stash of hashish brownies, 25 bottles of liquor, and a large amount of stolen prescription narcotics.

Their station now secure, the Coasties provided medical treatment to those injured in the storm and comfort to those people who had sought refuge at the Coast Guard outpost. With the malcontents detained, the Coasties fed everybody from their own limited supplies. Then they moved all sixty-three people to a safer location and transferred them to the Jefferson Parish Sheriff's deputies.

Now able to focus on the mission at hand, the Coasties began to clean up and prepare for operations. The entire city of New Orleans was without electrical power, so first on the list was firing up the emergency generator. It started and ran very well for about thirty minutes before it died. It had been installed several years before, had received regular maintenance, and had been run every month. But this day, when it was needed most, it failed most inconveniently. But the One-Armed Bandit, as Mike was popularly known at the station, was there with *Mañana*, and his generator was running. Always willing to help, Mike ran a power line from *Mañana* to the station and provided basic electricity to the station. Mike also had satellite TV, and he ran a cable for this as well, so for the first time the Coasties at the station could see what was happening in their city.

These young men and women, all under twenty-five years old, had spent the last four days evacuating, surviving the storm, hacking their way back to the water, launching their boats, and getting back to the station. Once there, they had to regain control, round up the looters, and try to get things running again. But like everybody else in New Orleans, all they knew of the storm's destruction was what they could see with their own eyes. They had had no access to television, radio was spotty, and cell phones were almost useless. Everybody knew things were bad, but nobody really knew how bad. With Mike's satellite TV, they could see for the first time the extent of the flooding throughout the city. They could see people stranded, and they knew this was the challenge of a lifetime. This was what they had trained for.

They immediately turned to rescuing people stranded on the lake side of the levee. They focused on lake operations because even the smallest of the station boats was a heavy twenty-one-foot rigid hull inflatable, far too large for use in the streets of the city. It was hot work. They were filthy from their efforts and hungry as well. Much of the station was unusable from the looters and the comforts of civilization weren't available, nor would they be for quite some time. But then Mike on *Mañana* gave them a shower and hot food, their first in a couple of days. The One-Armed Bandit came through again when he was needed most.

This kind old guy with a ready smile, this larger-than-life war vet who used to make them all laugh when he used his fake arm to stir a boiling pot of crawfish in happier times, this slightly eccentric guy with the dogs on his old fishing boat became a hero once again. He made it possible for Coast Guard Station New Orleans to return to rescue operations when it was needed most. As with the Cuban boat lift years before, Mike was exactly the right guy, at the right place, at the right time to serve a higher purpose. But the One-Armed Bandit wasn't finished yet.

Five Little Ones

Adam Jenkins and Courtney Hall were young petty officers working at Coast Guard Sector Upper Mississippi Valley when Katrina hit New Orleans. Sector Upper Miss, as it is known in the service, is based in St. Louis, Missouri, and both were members of a Disaster Assistance Response Team, a DART. The DART teams use small aluminum johnboats, sometimes called flood punts, to rescue people trapped by the periodic floods along the upper Mississippi River. You see them every few years on the television news maneuvering their boats down flooded streets when the river rises rapidly in response to heavy snow melts and extended rains. During these situations, the DARTs move into action, the little boats often going house to house rescuing people trapped by the flooding river. The teams are quite popular and well respected by the residents of those towns they protect. The DARTs are part of important missions, always assisted by local state police, sheriff's offices, and police departments, and these operations run smoothly. They are an excellent example of coordination between the community and various government agencies; they are well organized, practiced in advance, and well coordinated.

When Katrina hit and the levees failed, Coast Guard members up and down the river system, and, indeed, across the country, began making their way to New Orleans to help. The DART teams would be particularly useful in a flooded city, and they were among the first Coast Guard crews dispatched. The afternoon before the storm hit, Jenkins and Hall had been ordered to begin their preparations, and the next morning the two petty officers and their DART team loaded their trucks and boats onto a Coast Guard HC-130 airplane for the trip to Alexandria, Louisiana. They spent the night there and very early the next morning, they drove down to New Orleans.

Getting into the city was the first challenge to overcome. From the east, the main highway into New Orleans, Interstate 10, was gone. The massive "Twin Span" elevated bridge had been washed away by the storm surge. Interstate 10 west of New Orleans was underwater and would be for some time. Fortunately, the Causeway Bridge, a twenty-four-mile elevated causeway spanning Lake Pontchartrain on the city's north side, still stood, being just barely tall enough to avoid being washed away by the rising waters. This was the road the DART teams used to get into New Orleans.

Once in New Orleans, the scene they found was surreal,

Coast Guard DART teams convoying to New Orleans. (USCG)

like a bad movie gone horribly wrong. The first thing all the rescue teams noticed was that everyone was gone; much of the city seemed deserted. Shops and businesses were shuttered. There was no electricity, so no lights, no sound. People don't realize how much sound our modern world makes, but in the aftermath of Katrina, it was eerily silent, and the silence itself was disturbing. No cars, no trucks, no trains, no ships on the river, no music, no laughter, no air-conditioners, no construction cranes, no TVs, no radios. It was like a blanket of silence had descended upon the city. In the eerie stillness, however, certain sounds pierced the quiet and were magnified: crying children, people begging for help, screams of pain, and the occasional gunshot ringing out. Some areas downtown experienced looting and thus quite a bit of sound and activity, but in most neighborhoods, it was quiet and unsettling, at least at first.

Petty Officer Adam Jenkins was a Machinery Technician Third Class, or MK3, meaning he was trained in keeping engines running, in both maintenance and repair. But for this operation he was the coxswain, an ancient and honorable title meaning he was in charge of the boat, driving the boat and deciding what he and his crew should or should not do. Coast Guardsmen and -women are trained to make decisions on their own. When they are on a rescue mission, nobody can see their situation as well as they can, and while an operations center can offer advice over the radio, the Coastie on scene is expected to use good judgment and get the job done, safely and effectively. Jenkins, only a few years out of high school, found himself making life or death decisions, over and over and over again. His boat crew member was an MST3, a Marine Science Technician Third Class. MST3 Courtney Hall, also a very young petty officer, only two years out of high school, was trained in marine science, oil spills, and environmental protection. But right now she comprised the crew of the sixteen-foot flood punt. She would later serve as a coxswain as well. As might be expected in a rapidly expanding rescue operation, she was almost immediately an experienced "old hand" as new Coasties flooded into what was very rapidly becoming a massive rescue effort.

They arrived after the storm, on Day Two, and they drove downtown to a casino serving as a makeshift police headquarters. They picked up a police officer guide, who led the convoy to work in the Lower Ninth Ward, one of New Orleans' older neighborhoods, which was now completely underwater. Most of the residents were still in shock this early in the rescue operation. Their city had flooded, their houses were flooded, electricity was gone, phones didn't work, their food and water were downstairs in the kitchen, underwater, and they were cut off from their families, news, and all information. Entire neighborhoods were practically obliterated. Corner grocery stores, restaurants, barber shops, hair salons, schools, lounges, juke joints, churches, everything that represented normal was gone. All they knew was that their lives were suddenly and profoundly different,

DART teams carrying the flood punts to the water. (USCG)

death was a real possibility, and they were trapped with no help in sight.

It was a strange contrast to some parts of the city, such as the French Quarter, which was built on high ground and saw little damage. There, people were celebrating their survival of the storm in typical New Orleans fashion. Other areas that remained dry were soon beset by criminal types who noticed that the police were few and far between. And unfortunately, some of them started to look for what they could loot and how they could turn the situation to their own advantage. But in the flooded areas, which would prove to be most of New Orleans, the people were still in shock.

Jenkins and Hall launched their boat near the base of the St. Claude Avenue Bridge and steered into the flooded areas, but just navigating the former streets was a real challenge. Trees and power poles were down everywhere, and while power to the lines was mostly out, an occasional shower of sparks could make things interesting. Submerged cars could bring the boat to an immediate and sudden stop or tear up the engine. And cars were not the only obstacles hidden by the muddy floodwaters. There were jagged metal edges waiting to rip the bottom out of their thin-skinned aluminum boat and chunks of debris large enough to break their propeller and render the boat a raft. So many dangers, seen and unseen, to be avoided. Trash dumpsters, trailers, metal tanks, fallen and sunken trees, poles of various types, remnants of roofs, and other debris from houses and buildings all loomed unseen below the flood line. It took every bit of skill both of these young people possessed, Hall watching the water and peering ahead to see what might be lurking just beneath the surface to snag the boat, and Jenkins avoiding what he could see and steering as directed around obstacles he couldn't see. Like every Coast Guard boat crew, Jenkins and Hall quickly became a well-oiled machine. And as is always the case in dangerous situations, their lives depended on each other and team work.

DART boats getting underway for rescue operations. (USCG, PA1 Bauman)

On that first day these two young Coasties rescued eighty people from flooded housing units. There were thousands of people in the area, many in the water trying to get into the boats and others in the buildings waving and shouting for help. To help the weakest who were most at risk, Adam and Courtney decided to rescue children and their families and the elderly first. Consequently, most of their rescues that first day were young children or older people with medical problems. Their very first rescue involved five young children and one adult trapped on the second story of a housing complex. The kids were very young, ranging in age from a toddler to an eight year old, with four of the children under the age of five. In this area, the water was too deep to wade through but not deep enough to let the boat easily reach the second-story window. Jenkins could see the children in the window, and he had to drive his boat around a sunken car and a pile of debris to position the boat under the window.

The children inside were terrified; the world had come apart in their little eyes. The lights and television were off, and it was dangerously hot without the air-conditioner. None of their electric toys worked, and the batteries had died on the others. They were thirsty and hungry but their mother couldn't cook anything, and she was really upset. Almost everything they knew was underwater, and the neighbors in the building were acting strangely. *Everybody* was acting strangely. They could hear sporadic gunfire, and it wasn't TV gunfire; it was the real kind and they knew that was bad. And now, in the midst of all this chaos, these two strange people wanted them to climb out a window, get into an orange boat, and leave their home behind. The eight year old thought it might be fun. The younger ones, not a chance.

But the Coasties knew the dangers. They knew things were going to get a lot worse and they needed to get these kids to safety. So they began talking to the children, with Hall talking to the younger ones and their mother about getting into the boat. Chances are these kids had never been on a boat. These two strangers seemed pretty nice, their mom was talking to them, and slowly they started to think it might be okay. They needed some fun after all they had been through the past couple of days. Jenkins used the boat hook to pull down the ladder for the fire escape while Hall coaxed each child down the ladder and into her waiting arms. Once all the children and their mother were safely onboard, they carefully drove the boat to a makeshift landing alongside part of the interstate that wasn't flooded. Once they reached the landing, other Coasties ushered the family to safety.

While the rescue boats were shuttling survivors to the interstate, helicopters were operating from this staging point as well, delivering those rescued from rooftops to dry land. One unexpected problem with the proximity of helicopters was the rotor wash. When a helicopter flies, it sends a tremendous wash of air downwards, called the rotor wash, which can be a problem if you are in a sixteen-foot johnboat loaded down with people as a helicopter flies fifteen feet over your head. In one case Jenkins and Hall were heading in with two women and a baby onboard. A helicopter came in low and the rotor wash was very heavy, blowing things everywhere. Hall remembered a pair of coveralls in a bag onboard, and she quickly unzipped the bag, took out the coveralls, and shoved the baby inside. She then clung to him for dear life. It felt like the hurricane blast of rotor wash was going to shove them all out of the boat and into the water. The helicopter soon passed, the baby was unscathed, and the rescues continued.

Jenkins and Hall made many other rescues that Tuesday. They found a sixteen-year-old girl and her four-month-old baby on a rapidly sinking raft. Jenkins quickly maneuvered his boat alongside the capsizing raft while Hall grabbed the baby and young mother and pulled them to safety. Overall the DART teams rescued an estimated 750 people that first day in and around the totally flooded Lower Ninth Ward.

To maximize the number of rescues, Coasties from Station New Orleans would meet the little DART boats in quickly designated areas, tie up together, and transfer the people from the little flood punts to larger boats. The larger boats would then shuttle the people to the St. Claude Avenue Bridge landing while the flood punts went back to the houses for more survivors. Once rescued and on dry land, the rescuees were taken by the National Guard to shelter in the Superdome, where they received food and water. Many of these people would later need to be rescued from the Superdome, but on the first days of these life-saving water rescues, the Superdome was a beacon of hope.

By the end of their first day, Jenkins and Hall were exhausted, as were the crews of the other DART boats that had come down from St. Louis. As darkness fell, they returned to their makeshift landing, trailered their boats, and started to look for a safe place to spend the night. They climbed into the trucks and headed to the Navy base, Naval Support Activity East Bank, but the convoy became spread out due to the nearly impassable conditions of the roads. Their heavy trucks and trailers had to work their way through and around many obstacles. Often they had to stop and clear the road to get the boat trailers through. By the time Petty Officers Jenkins and Hall arrived at the base, they couldn't reach the gate due to the rioting crowd just outside. Some of the rioters had recently been rescued from the water, but they had been left behind when the bus transport to the Superdome stopped around 5:00 P.M., and they felt abandoned. Getting anything working in the devastated city was a monumental effort, and without doubt the bus operators had a host of challenges to overcome to keep the evacuation moving. The rioters couldn't realize that; they were just angry and scared. Seeing the danger at the Navy base and realizing they could not get inside the gate, the exhausted Coast Guard crew slowly made their way out of the city to Baton Rouge, where they spent the night in a shelter for rescue workers.

They were back the next morning, driving their boats house to house, building to building, helping people in desperate need. At the end of a very long day, Jenkins and Hall rescued some older gentlemen and overheard them talking about an ill elderly man who only had two hours of oxygen left in his oxygen tank. It was a long way back to the building, and it was quickly getting dark, a very dangerous time to be out. The rules for the operation required all boats to be in by dark, as some lawless individuals were starting to shoot at law enforcement and rescue personnel. But Jenkins and Hall knew what had to be done; they were driven by a deep need to help others. After delivering their passengers to safety, they turned the boat around, found the building in the dark, and rescued the older man whose oxygen was indeed running out. He surely would have died without their complete disregard for their own safety and intense concern for his.

In those first critical days, the young Coasties operated alone in an increasingly hostile environment. As the disaster progressed and the levels of fear in the city rose, Jenkins and Hall found that the flooded city was providing new dangers. The people they were trying to rescue were sometimes proving to be a threat as well. The conditions the survivors faced were degenerating. Without food and water for days, they were getting slowly cooked by the heat inside the buildings, where temperatures often reached 115 degrees, and many were scared by the gunfire they heard around them.

As the initial shock wore off, the criminal element became increasingly violent and mobile. Unfortunately, the New Orleans Police Department presence was greatly reduced by the storm. Many had reported to their local police stations before the hurricane but were sent home to ride it out, the idea being that they would report for duty as soon as the weather had passed. This was a good plan in the case of a typical hurricane, a response that had worked for decades of storms. But as the floodwaters came rushing in, many of the police officers were trapped in their flooded houses, victims like most everybody else in the city. So the criminals and the looters found themselves in a unique situation: there was no one to stop their illicit behavior. It's not that New Orleans is worse than, say, New York or Miami. Every major city has its violent criminal element. As is the case in any large city, if you take the police out of the picture, the criminals will run wild. And they did in New Orleans.

As might be expected, alarmed citizens began to arm themselves in self-defense, and sometimes they shot at anybody they didn't know. Occasionally that might inadvertently include rescue personnel. Some of the criminals decided to take advantage of the situation to go after their rival criminal groups and expand their territory, and a lot of them shot each other. But sometimes rescuers ended up in the crossfire. Some of the criminals even decided to go after law enforcement personnel directly. These two-legged predators liked things the way they were and clearly did not want the return of law and order. You could see it in their eyes; these were the most dangerous. In the course of the emergency operation, Petty Officer Hall would become coxswain of her own boat and have to dodge sniper fire. Fortunately she reacted quickly and skillfully maneuvered her boat out of harm's way. Her experience was not unique; other boats would also become targets of snipers.

In those first, very long, and seemingly endless days when thousands of rescues were made, the only law enforcement presence—and indeed the only government presence at all—was often the Coast Guard in their little orange boats. Rescue was the priority, but staying alive was important too. After the first day or two, as threats emerged, the Coast Guard not only armed the crews but also deployed heavily armed Maritime Safety and Security Team (MSST) members on the little boats. The MSST guys helped tremendously. They provided a visual presence that deterred the criminals. But from the very start, when they didn't have security support, and even later when they did, those young eighteen-, nineteen-, and twenty-year-old Coasties proved their courage every day. These dedicated souls knew the dangers—they saw them firsthand—yet they went back again and again. They entered a free-for-all environment full of danger: submerged dangers lurking and waiting to destroy their boats and leave them stranded; dangers in the water itself, which was becoming more polluted by the day; and dangers from criminals as well as terrified, well-meaning innocents.

Living conditions after a long day on the water were tough as well. Supplies of every kind were being rushed to New Orleans, but resources were limited for a long time. By the time the last of the boat crews got in, the food was pretty thin, and getting clean was impossible in those early days. Courtney Hall remembers one National Guard member who gave several of the women a few gallons of water and then blocked off an area so that they could wash their hair. She later said it was the ultimate luxury, and with her hair about three feet long, it was greatly appreciated.

Working closely with each other, the Coasties found ways to keep each other going under these difficult conditions. Brandon Miller, a Damage Control Specialist, excelled at this. He would fix the trailers and boats every day, keeping things running. He was also a master scrounger, finding things that were needed to keep the operation moving. But perhaps most importantly, he listened to problems and helped when he could. There were many like him, the oil that kept the rescue machine running. But spirits were high; the Coast Guard men and women hardly knew they were roughing it. And their sacrifices were making a huge difference, saving hundreds of lives.

It takes a lot to risk your life for a loved one. It takes more to risk your life for a friend. And to deliberately risk your life, to put yourself in grave danger, for a complete stranger is to show intense personal courage and a true love for your fellow man. To do it again and again and again is beyond most all of us. Like all the other young Coasties running rescue boats in the city, I doubt Petty Officers Adam Jenkins and Courtney Hall considered themselves heroes. They will tell you they were just doing their jobs, what they had been trained to do. And thank God they did, because undoubtedly they were the answer to many desperate prayers.

The Soup Bowl

The land that would become New Orleans was formed over thousands of years by the outflow of the Mississippi River, aptly named the "Father of Waters" by the Indians who had lived along the banks of the great river for centuries. The river provided food, water, transportation, and a way of life for the many tribes along its banks from Minnesota to New Orleans. The rhythms of its rising and falling guided their lives through the seasons. As it had always done, the river overflowed its banks each year, spreading sediment that washed down from the Great Plains over the swamps and bayous, slowly building them up, creating new land. The lower part of Louisiana that extends out into the Gulf of Mexico is land formed by the constant flooding of the river and the resulting sediment deposit. And this sediment, washed down from Iowa, Tennessee, and all the other states along the Mississippi and Ohio River basins, is excellent soil, making Louisiana farms along the river very productive.

French explorers, traders, and trappers began to arrive in the area that would be called New Orleans in the 1680s and 1690s, and in 1700, French settlers began to build the first military base, though that term was somewhat optimistic. Fort St. Jean, later anglicized to Fort St. John, was built on a mound of oyster shells discarded by the Indians near Bayou St. John. Later upgraded by the Spanish, the area is known today as Spanish Fort. To the original French explorers and settlers, the area had significant strategic advantages. In the race to acquire territory in the New World, the French had been latecomers to the party but had done well in staking out territory in Canada, the Gulf Coast, and the interior of the North American continent. The British held the valuable east coast, with its significant industries in fisheries, agriculture, and trade. The British also claimed parts of Canada, though much of that territory was unexplored and its value unknown. The Spanish held rich lands in Mexico and Central and South America, dotted with gold and silver mines, along with various Caribbean islands and much of what is today the American West, though that hold was tenuous at best. While there didn't seem to be any gold or silver in the French areas, nor the rich fisheries and agriculture the British colonies enjoyed, the French-held territory was huge and had tremendous, if untapped, potential. With the French claiming most of the American heartland, the Mississippi River was the natural highway into this largely unexplored and seemingly endless region larger than France itself, and controlling the mouth of this river was essential to maintaining the French claim.

The problem was that much of the land within about ninety miles of the mouth of the Mississippi River was and is marshy and swampy, subject to frequent flooding. There was no place suitable to build a settlement or a decent fort on solid ground, safe from the threat of floods. Still, the mouth of the river had to be settled and defended if the French were to hold on to their claim to large portions of North America. In 1718, Jean-Baptiste Le Moyne de Bienville founded La Nouvelle-Orléans on the east bank of the Mississippi River and, with his own future clearly in mind, named it for the man next in line for the throne of France, Phillip II, the Duke of Orléans. He located what he expected to be a bustling city about one hundred miles upriver from the mouth of the river, on the only suitable high ground he could find. The original city was sited on a natural levee built by the river itself, and local Indians had once settled there. It was an inspired choice, for in its long and storied history, the French Quarter, very near where Bienville established what we know as New Orleans, has rarely flooded and never seriously.

The reason is obvious to any river rat who has ever worked a boat on the Mississippi River. Bienville established his city just downriver from what we know today as Algiers Point, a very sharp bend in the river where the Mississippi turns almost back on itself. Such a sharp bend makes the far bank a natural settling place for sediment, a natural building place for land to slowly develop. That long crescent-shaped area soon became known as the Crescent City and boasted the first high ground coming upriver from the Gulf of Mexico.

That same sharp bend also provided an excellent place from which to control the river, and defense was a very important consideration for what was to be the capital of the new French colony. To the west and south, the Spanish had been in Mexico for nearly two hundred years and were well established both militarily and economically. The Spanish were also in Florida to the east and were thought to have an eye on the French claim in Louisiana as a way of tying their two colonies together and gaining control of the entire area, as well as the heartland of the continent. While the British on the east coast were farther away than the Spanish, the British colonies could be used as a base for colonial expansion. With the prosperity and capability of the nearby British Colonies, and the tremendous strength of the Royal Navy, Bienville's placement of the city was militarily strategic. It would have been very difficult for a sailing ship of the day to make the sharp turn at Algiers Point and then sail past the long crescent of New Orleans without being sunk by gunfire. This fact effectively gave the French complete control of the river. Since travel over land for any real distance by wagon in this wilderness was nearly impossible, the French control of Algiers Point effectively gave them a stranglehold on much of the interior of North America from the Appalachian Mountains and across the Great Plains.

In 1722, New Orleans was made the capital of French Louisiana, replacing Biloxi, Mississippi. Later that year, a hurricane flattened the new capital, and the city leaders rebuilt on a grid plan that can still be seen in the French Quarter today. While the Mississippi River continued to flood nearly every year, the new French city of New Orleans remained a good area to live and work. Unfortunately it wasn't very profitable for its colonizers. The French weren't making any money exporting agricultural products out of New Orleans and in 1763 transferred the settlement to Spain in the Treaty of Paris. This treaty ended what was then a world war involving all the great European powers of the day, a war recorded in our history books as the French and Indian War and won by the British. This was the war where a young Colonel George Washington of the British Virginia Militia first gained the military experience that would prove so valuable in the American Revolution some thirteen years later.

In the 1763 Treaty of Paris, Britain won the French territory east of the Mississippi River, and Spain got the river itself, New Orleans, and the French territory west of the Mississippi River. In reality, though, France had secretly transferred New Orleans to Spain just before the treaty was written. New Orleans grew under Spanish rule, and English-speaking settlers began coming into the city as a result of trade with the now neighborly British colonies. After the American Revolution, the Americans began moving into what we now know as Kentucky and other areas west of the Allegheny Mountains, but the difficulty in moving their farm goods back over the mountains to market kept settlements small and isolated. The 1783 Treaty of Paris gave the new United States access to the Mississippi River and the port of New Orleans, allowing Americans to send their goods downriver. With the tributaries of both the Ohio and Mississippi Rivers spread throughout the American territories east of the Mississippi River, it was like having a maritime highway system, all flowing into this superhighway to the sea and the major seaport of New Orleans. Their trade route guaranteed, the Americans territories grew rapidly.

In 1800, Spain agreed to return New Orleans and the

Louisiana Territory to France in exchange for a small kingdom in Italy. In 1802 the transfer was made, and the new French owners cut off American access to the warehouses and the port of New Orleans. This was a national crisis for the Americans, for without access to the river, the American "western territories," as they were known at the time, the settlements in Kentucky, Tennessee, Arkansas, West Virginia, Ohio, and others, would all die a slow financial death without a way to export their crops, furs, and other products. Worse for the Americans was the threat of their domineering new neighbor. Having a weak Spain next door wasn't really a problem for the brand-new United States, but sharing borders with a very powerful France was another matter indeed. Having just fought the undeclared "Quasi-War" with France in 1798, the Americans were worried the new leader of France, Napoleon Bonaparte, might have designs on American territory or even the entire American nation.

Fortunately for the Americans, Napoleon had troubles of his own. Haiti, his most valuable colony, was in the midst of an ongoing slave revolt, and the army he sent to suppress it was decimated by yellow fever. The islands in the Caribbean were incredibly valuable at the time for their sugar plantations, and Haiti was the jewel in the French crown. In a time when food generally tasted bland and was often half-spoiled, sugar was more profitable than oil is today and those islands that produced it were national treasures for their European masters. With the fighting in Haiti and the collapse of his army in the Caribbean, Napoleon realized he could not hold and defend the massive and rather empty territory of Louisiana without draining forces he would really rather use in his upcoming conquest of Europe. So he sold it to the fledgling United States in 1803 in the land deal of the century. With this fifteen-million-dollar purchase, President Thomas Jefferson effectively doubled the size of his nation.

In 1803, New Orleans had approximately 8,000 residents, including 4,000 whites, 2,700 slaves, and 1,300 free persons of color. As an American city, New Orleans' population quickly grew and the city's boundaries were forced to expand with the influx of newcomers. At first, most of the population was centered around the French Quarter. As more Americans arrived, they established their own community, stretching from Canal Street through the Garden District and Uptown, on the high ground near the river. This American sector was bounded by the river on one side and surrounded by swampy areas on the other. By 1850 there were more than 115,000 people living in New Orleans, and it was growing fast despite the challenges posed by the lack of suitable land on which to build. By 1900, nearly 300,000 people called New Orleans home, and it was by far the largest and most important seaport on the Gulf Coast and one of the most important cities in America. The city would continue to expand, and it is in the expansion since 1900 that the seeds of the Katrina disaster were first planted.

In the aftermath of Katrina, the local paper, the *Times-Picayune,* ran a map of New Orleans from the 1890s. I was struck by the fact that none of the areas of New Orleans that were inhabited in 1890 had flooded. It was only those areas developed after 1890 that were flooded by Katrina.

As the city grew, more land was urgently required. To meet this need, swamps were drained and land was reclaimed. To drain the swamps, canals leading into Lake Pontchartrain were dug throughout the city. Water was pumped into the lake through this system of canals, which also served as drainage during severe rain events or when the river reached unusually high levels.

The reclamation of the swamp land benefited the citizens of New Orleans in another important way. The swamps were a breeding ground for millions of the mosquitoes that carried malaria, yellow fever, and dengue fever, deadly diseases that periodically ravaged New Orleans. Fewer swamps meant fewer places for the mosquito to live and breed. Though mosquitoes will always be a problem in Louisiana because it rains so much, with the elimination of the swamps, the mosquito population in New Orleans went from being unspeakably bad to being just a serious nuisance.

Unfortunately, there were also serious downsides to the swamp reclamation projects. In many areas the elevation of the reclaimed land was lower than the water level in the lake. Obviously this was a problem, and earthen levees were built on the shore of the lake to provide flood protection for the new neighborhoods. These levees were simply a series of long dirt mounds running the length of the lake's shore and provided good protection even if the lake should rise significantly. The drainage canals had flood-wall levees built along their sides as well, and these were also designed to contain a flood condition in the lake. The various levees along the lake, as well as the levees along the river itself, were built up dramatically after the Great Mississippi River Flood of 1927. The improved system worked well, and with a few exceptions, the areas inside the levees were kept dry year after year.

One unintended side effect of all these levees was that New Orleans now resembled a giant soup bowl. The city was surrounded by walls to keep the water out, and events were to prove the walls could also keep water in. While the French Quarter and nearby areas were about six feet above sea level, some parts of the city were ten or even fifteen feet below sea level. Yet the system of pumps and levees did its job, and the citizens began to forget the threat that water could pose.

But in 2005, Hurricane Katrina completely overwhelmed the levees and pumping system. The same canals that drained the water out of the swamps and into Lake Pontchartrain now became conduits for water flowing from the storm-swollen lake directly into the city. As the water quickly rose in the lake, the water rushed into the canals, proved too much for the pumping system, and broke through the flood walls protecting those neighborhoods that had once been swamps.

The 17th Street Canal itself was built deep into the Bucktown and Lakeview neighborhoods and was originally used to drain the land for development. This canal, like several others throughout the city, was now used to direct water from heavy rains away from the neighborhoods and into the lake with the help of large pumps. And like the other canals, the one at 17th Street was now rapidly filling with massive amounts of water forced into it by the heavily swollen Lake Pontchartrain. When the I-wall levee broke on the Lakeview side, muddy water crashed through homes in a huge rushing wave. The canal would prove deadly for those same neighborhoods it was supposed to protect.

A similar scenario played out throughout the city, flooding neighborhoods in the Lower and Upper Ninth Wards, Treme, Gentilly, City Park, Mid-City, Broadmoor, Arabi, New Orleans East, and Chalmette. Many people who had stayed behind to

The sunken state of humanity. (USCG, PA1 Bauman)

ride out the storm found themselves trapped as water invaded their communities and turned their homes into islands. The lucky ones made it up to their dark and very hot attics or managed to crawl out onto their rooftops to signal for help. Others drowned as the floodwaters rushed in.

The flooded areas of the city reached parity with the level of the lake by September 1, two days after the storm made landfall, and some neighborhoods would remain underwater for weeks. A "bathtub ring" marked the city, the sludge remaining even after the water slowly drained away. It would be years before the last of this bathtub ring would be scrubbed away. What is not commonly understood is that the ring of mud and debris inscribed on homes and businesses represents where the water level equalized. During the height of the flood, when the lake was swollen with Katrina's storm surge, the water level was in fact much higher in many parts of the city. In some cases, the floodwaters crested over ten feet higher than the bathtub ring, as evidenced by photographs of boats and other debris piled on top of houses that rose quite a bit above the standing water level. But the ring was a good reminder for years that the soup bowl proved as good at keeping water in as it did at keeping it out.

Who Picked Alexandria?

Long before Hurricane Katrina was a superstorm, or even a thunderstorm, Coast Guard officers in New Orleans had been planning their response to a major hurricane. It's what we do living and working on the Gulf Coast. Coasties have been planning for hurricanes in Louisiana since 1820, when the first two Revenue Cutters, the *Louisiana* and the *Alabama,* fought pirates at the mouth of the Mississippi River, the Revenue Cutter Service being the forerunner of today's Coast Guard.

Every mariner on the Gulf Coast knows you have to plan for hurricanes. When the 120-mile-per-hour winds of a Category 3 hurricane roar ashore, along with the thirty-foot seas such storms often bring, vessels in the river, moored at docks, anchored, or even underway near the coast are in grave danger. The lesser Category 1 storms are fairly common, and with winds between 74 and 95 miles per hour, they can be destructive yet are rarely catastrophic.

It seems there is a threat of a Category 1 storm every few years, and residents along the Gulf Coast go through the drill. Stores are emptied of bread and milk, gas tanks are filled and generators tested, and some people in low-lying areas like Grand Isle may evacuate. But for the most part, the Cat 1 storms provide great entertainment as people keep an eye on the Weather Channel to watch the storm track and then discuss it with friends and family, trying to guess where it is going and whether or not it will strengthen. Local radio and television airwaves are filled with experts providing opinions and detailing consequences, discussing all the options, both realistic and not. If a Cat 1 hits, damage is caused and everybody is reminded that things can be dangerous for those living on the coast. Make no mistake, if a Category 1 hurricane stalls out over an area, the sustained winds of around 90 miles per hour and flooding from days of torrential rain can lead to total devastation. But usually the smaller hurricane moves on through, leaving notable but repairable damage in its path.

Category 2 storms, with winds between 96 and 110 miles per hour, get more interesting. Now everybody is glued to the Weather Channel, as a Cat 2 might make the jump to a Cat 3. And a Category 3 storm, officially a major hurricane, is serious business indeed. If a Cat 3 is coming, people begin to consider evacuating, bread and milk are long gone from grocery store shelves, and preparations get serious. Homeowners start the laborious process of boarding up their windows, driving Sheetrock screws into their window frames as they secure thick plywood over the glass. The quarter-inch stuff won't cut it. Some use those new clips guaranteed to withstand 150-mile-per-hour winds, but many prefer the secure feeling that driving the screws home gives. The windows are covered to withstand wind-blown hazards. A lawn chair or poolside table can become a missile in 120-mile-per-hour winds, so they all have to be put away. As the old joke goes, "You know you live on the Gulf Coast when the pool furniture looks good at the bottom of the pool." It's safe there and takes up less room than in the garage. Everything in the yard must be cleared and put inside, and better check the neighbor's yard as well. His stuff could come flying through your window.

The Coast Guard, just like everyone else on the Gulf Coast, must go through this pre-storm preparation, with the caveat that the Coasties must be on the job, fully operational, right after the hurricane passes. Unlike the homeowner who can wait a couple of weeks to take down the plywood, fish the lawn furniture out of the pool, and drag the potted plants out of the living room, Coasties have to be ready to go as soon as the storm passes, and sometimes before. People will need saving, ships will be in danger, oil will be spilled, and the Coast Guard must be ready to spring into action as soon as the winds die down. This makes preparation much more challenging. All boats and personnel must be safe, secure, protected, yet ready for immediate action. The Coast Guard Sector New Orleans plan for Katrina was a combination of two very different plans, because two very different Coast Guard organizations worked in New Orleans until a few days before the storm, as they had done for decades. In addition, Air Station New Orleans had its own hurricane plan, which by necessity was a very different plan in itself due to the nature of aviation.

Captain Frank Paskewich was the Commanding Officer of Coast Guard Marine Safety Office New Orleans and as such he was the Captain of the Port, a time-honored and very meaningful title. He was responsible for the lower section of the Mississippi River, from north of Baton Rouge to its outlet at the Gulf of Mexico, more than two hundred miles away, and he was responsible for the Port of New Orleans, Port of Baton Rouge, Port of South Louisiana, Port of Plaquemines, and the Port of St. Bernard. These five ports along the Mississippi River effectively constitute one very long port complex and as such form one of the largest, busiest, and most successful ports in the world. Captain Paskewich and his staff ensured the safety of both the vessels and the port facilities on and along the river.

Though they were tasked with ensuring that everything on the river operated safely and securely, the Marine Safety Office (MSO) had few boats. In fact, there is no Coast Guard boat station on the river. The lower Mississippi River doesn't even have boat ramps because of the large rise and fall of the river stage, and the river itself has tremendous current when it is up and running hard. The Marine Safety Office Coasties did their work from trucks and via telephone. When necessary, they rode with one of the many crew boats operating on the

Captain Frank Paskewich (right), the Sector Commander, and CWO Dan Brooks, Commanding Officer of Station New Orleans. Captain Paskewich was the overall Coast Guard Commander and would focus his Katrina efforts on reopening the vital Mississippi River for trade while dealing with massive oil spills and beginning the largest salvage operation ever attempted in the United States. Chief Warrant Officer Brooks would reopen his battered rescue station and host more than five hundred personnel from all over the Coast Guard as part of the largest search and rescue operation ever conducted. (USCG, Mike Howell)

river. They could also catch a ride on Coast Guard helicopters from Air Station New Orleans or the occasional Coast Guard small boat scheduled to be on the river. For a Coast Guard small boat to operate on the Mississippi, it has to navigate from Station New Orleans on Lake Pontchartrain, through the Industrial Canal, and into the river, a process that typically takes about an hour. Whether working from trucks, boats, or helicopters, MSO New Orleans had a monumental task, with more than eight thousand ships on the river every year, not to mention tens of thousands of barges.

While New Orleans is only a minor container port when compared to Long Beach, California, it moves nearly everything else shipped into and out of the country. About seventy-five percent of the entire U.S. grain harvest is shipped through New Orleans, coming downriver on barges to the New Orleans area. Usually the grain is transferred to a grain elevator ashore, and then to a ship, though sometimes it is transferred directly from the barges to large waiting cargo ships in a midstream transfer using very large floating cranes. One company, Associated Terminals, has a floating grain elevator that scoops the grain out of the barges and moves it to the ship, weighing it and measuring moisture content and quality in the process. To put it in perspective, a 42-barge tow, meaning one towboat pushing 42 barges, can carry the weight of 2,500 semi-trailer trucks or 630 railroad cars; and 42-barge tows are a common sight bringing grain down from St. Louis and points farther north to the ports of New Orleans, Baton Rouge, South Louisiana, Plaquemines, and St. Bernard. One cargo ship can take 60, 80, or even up to 120 barges in a single load, and ships from all over the world come to New Orleans to load grain. Then there is the coal export trade, sending tens of millions of tons overseas, as well as the fertilizer import trade, the chemical trade, the oil and gas trades, the iron ore trade, and countless others. The greater New Orleans area is a huge port system, vital to the economic health of the United States and, indeed, the world.

The height of the river, or "river stage," as it is known, is watched by shippers all around the world. It tells the ship owners how deep they can load their ships, how much cargo they can carry. The Army Corps of Engineers is charged with maintaining the main channel of the river at forty-five feet deep, and they work year-round to fulfill this duty. But it isn't easy. The river rises and falls all year long in response to snow melt, rainfall, and drought. Every weather event in the twenty states that drain into the Mississippi River, from Montana and South Dakota in the west to Minnesota and Pennsylvania in the east, has an effect. When the river is high and running fast, whether from a heavy snow melt or extended rain in the Ohio Valley, it carries massive amounts of sediment, and the Corps has to dredge more to keep the channel clear. If the river suddenly drops, it is even worse, as all the sediment settles out of the slower-moving water, which combined with the lower water level means even more dredging. These wide-ranging changes make monitoring the river stage so very important for shipping.

Let's say you are the owner of a very large cargo ship, one that draws around forty-five feet of water. If you can load that ship with enough tons of corn so that the ship draws forty-seven feet of water, that extra cargo means more profit, because you are paid by the ton and your fixed costs associated with the ship don't change much. But if the river has shallow spots that haven't been dredged out yet and you can only safely load your ship to forty-three feet deep, you might be losing money. Even though you are carrying less cargo, you still have to pay the relatively fixed cost of fuel, crew salaries, and ship maintenance.

In America, most of us take for granted the "Mighty Mississippi," but we don't really understand the river, beyond what we have read of Huck Finn's adventures floating down it on a raft. This river is a major focus of ship owners and shipping agencies around the world. Our Mississippi River is *the* superhighway that goes right into the heart of America. Any stoppage of marine traffic will cost our economy nearly $400 million dollars a day and back up commerce from Minneapolis and St. Louis to Amsterdam and Shanghai. To be trusted with such a massive and important command speaks volumes about Captain Paskewich, and he lived up to that trust.

Captain Frank Paskewich is a 1981 graduate of the U.S. Coast Guard Academy in New London, Connecticut. The smallest of the four military service academies, in the late 1970s it was one of the toughest colleges in the nation. In the following class, graduating in 1982, more than 8,200 individuals applied, 310 were accepted, but only 144 graduated. Swab Summer, as boot camp was known, was an entire summer of pain and struggle, and many were quickly weeded out. After nearly two months of extreme physical exercise, mental gymnastics, and precious little sleep, the one-week summer cruise on the sailing ship *Eagle* was a welcome relief and, for many, an introduction to the sea. Onboard *Eagle,* the physical and mental training were put to good use, as human muscle and brains make the 295-foot ship sail. Whether hoisting a 3,520-pound upper topsail yard into place with fifty cadets pulling on the halyard and pulling or easing various sheets, clews, and bunts to set the sail or keeping track of 154 different lines working the rigging, in the dark, it is a challenge. And with the dangerous and elegant dance requiring the entire crew to tack the ship and move all 22 sails from one side of the ship to the other while moving the bow of the ship through the wind, every cadet is put to the test. As a former Commanding Officer of USCGC *Eagle,* Captain H. A. Paulsen, was once quoted in *Eagle Seamanship:* "There is no hiding from the elements nor oneself on a weather end of a yardarm 150 feet above the rolling sea. It is a moment of truth which each seaman must experience for himself."

Swab Summer and the brief *Eagle* cruise are followed by a short trip home, where all cadets regale their parents, siblings, and friends with tales of hard work, derring-do, and questionable food. Most parents notice quite a change in their child; their spoiled high-schooler has turned into somebody with grit, as they used to say. Then the new freshmen head back to the Academy for class, usually about seventeen to nineteen hours a semester, plus the required military drills and training, in addition to the required varsity sports two out of three seasons. The sports are a blessing, and since two out of three cadets were team captains in high school, it's

A large ship loading via midstream transfer from barges. (Associated Terminals)

The Coast Guard sail training ship Eagle, *where Coast Guard Officers are made. (USCG)*

pretty competitive. Paskewich excelled in soccer and could often be seen running around the Academy, training hard, with his trademark running style. Classes were brutal, and with every cadet being at the very top of his or her high-school class, competition was intense. Most went from straight As in high school to struggling for Cs, a real shock to the system. Freshman year continued the intense military training, with a lot of toilet scrubbing, floor waxing, and indoctrination, and little freedom of any kind. Upper class years were easier militarily but often even harder academically. But the Coast Guard wants a very specific kind of officer, and the forty-five percent or so who survived to graduate were pretty hard-core individuals who could accomplish just about anything.

Frank and I were in the same company at the Academy, with him being a year ahead of me. He was a very happy and easygoing soul, while polished and professional. He was a very good guy back then, and he hadn't changed at all when we met up again twenty-five years later in New Orleans.

Captain Mark Blace was the Commanding Officer of Coast Guard Group New Orleans, the other major Coast Guard command in the city. The Groups were known as Operations Ashore, or "Ops Ashore," because they ran the system of small boat rescue stations along the nation's coasts. Groups also ran the much larger 87- and 110-foot patrol boats stationed around the country as well as the aids to navigation teams and construction tenders that maintained the various aids, or sign posts, along the nation's waterways. While the Marine Safety Office focused on the commercial aspects of the Mississippi River and its ports, as well as the offshore oil fields in the Gulf, the Group focused on the rescue and law enforcement missions on the river, along the coastal waters, and on Lake Pontchartrain. The primary missions of the Groups were search and rescue, fisheries enforcement, drug enforcement, and maintenance of the aids to navigation so important to mariners navigating our waterways.

Group New Orleans had four small boat stations, each

with about four or five rescue boats, located in New Orleans, Venice, Grand Isle, and Gulfport, Mississippi. In addition, the Group had four of the sleek 87-foot patrol boats for various open ocean rescue and law enforcement missions. For search and rescue missions and other critical missions, the Group had immediate access to helicopters from Air Station New Orleans. Whenever a mariner was in distress in the Gulf, in the bayou, or on the lake, Group New Orleans would get the call and would launch a boat or helicopter as needed. Group New Orleans also had two construction tenders and four aids to navigation teams to keep the lights on the buoys and shore-side aids to navigation "winking and blinking" and the buoys and aids themselves in the proper position. This is an often unsung mission in the Coast Guard, but as we saw in Katrina, without the red and green buoys and dayboards marking the deep channel, marine traffic in general and shipping in particular comes to a rather sudden and complete halt. Nothing moves on the river unless the navigation aids are correctly positioned and fully operational.

These two different Coast Guard worlds, which focused on very different missions—the industry-focused Marine Safety Office and the rescue-focused Group—were scheduled to become one, a new entity to be called Sector New Orleans, at the end of August. That would prove to be quite a target date. Given the very high importance of the lower Mississippi River and the ports in the greater New Orleans area to the nation, the Marine Safety Office's Commanding Officer, Captain Frank Paskewich, would be the Sector Commander. This made perfect sense. The Group Commanding Officer, Captain Mark Blace, was retiring. I would relieve Captain Blace, become the Sector Deputy Commander, and serve as the expert in all things related to Operations Ashore, including rescue and maritime law enforcement operations. Frank was very gracious and let me run the former Group units and manage their issues as needed. Since the river is a very busy place, he was fully occupied anyway. There was a huge amount of work to be done to combine the MSO with the Group. These two units had different offices, the MSO being downtown in an office building across from the Louisiana Superdome and the Group headquarters being located on Lake Pontchartrain, co-located with Station New Orleans. Before the push to combine and become a Sector, many of the people in these two units barely knew each other, since they worked different missions in different locations. Coordination was good when needed, but that wasn't as often as you might think.

The hurricane plans themselves were quite different, as might be expected. The Group plan was complicated, yet easy. The idea is to get the boats away from the storm to safe locations then get them back when the storm has passed. Most Group hurricane plans were very similar, with only the sites of the specific safe areas varying to fit local conditions and geography. For Group New Orleans, the plan was to send the 41-foot rescue boats and the 55-foot aids to navigation boats upriver in a convoy with the river tender *Pamlico* to the Baton Rouge area where they would be safe. Smaller boats were trailered north of the lake or to other interior areas in Louisiana and Mississippi. Some vessels headed up the Pearl River, while some of the patrol boats were directed to Texas ports to avoid the worst of Hurricane Katrina. But no matter where they went to dodge or ride out the storm, whether afloat or ashore, all were expected to be ready for action after the storm passed. I had worked on similar plans at Group Mobile and in Puerto Rico at the Coast Guard base there. These plans are simple and effective.

The Marine Safety Office plan was a very different animal, as their task was nothing like the Group's. First, as initial warnings of the approaching storm came in, the MSO began a well-versed procedure in preparation of shutting the port down. With a port system the size of the five ports of the New Orleans area, that was a massive undertaking, involving hundreds of ships, brokers, companies, facilities, oil refineries, factories, shipyards, fleets, and other entities on and around the river. The complex plan covers every facility on the river, with specific people to contact and specific actions to take at specific times. For example, when the hurricane is 72 hours out, there is a huge list of things that must be done to prepare the port. When the hurricane is 48 hours out, another huge list of specific tasks comes into play. When the hurricane is 24 hours out, yet another very long list of tasks to complete is required. By 12 hours out, the list becomes much smaller as every vessel should be gone or heavily secured, all facilities just about shut down, and evacuations under way. These actions must be performed in a specific order as well, as some facilities need to be shut down and vessels moved out of canals by certain times so that bridges can be locked down to allow unrestricted vehicular flow for people evacuating in front of the storm and the evacuation of the bridge tenders themselves. It is a monumental undertaking to close down one of the largest port complexes in the world, and the plan needed to be exceptional to keep all vessels, facilities, oil refineries, and people safe.

In addition to the hurricane plan, Captain Frank Paskewich needed a Continuity of Operations Plan to keep Coast Guard operations going if New Orleans was destroyed or heavily impacted and he could not reopen and run river operations from his regular headquarters in downtown New Orleans. The Group, with only a very small headquarters staff and most of its personnel spread out in boat stations and on cutters throughout southern Louisiana and Mississippi, didn't need such a plan. The Group Commander and his staff could relocate to any of the stations that survived the storm. But the MSO had a very large and centrally located staff, and they would need a full suite of phones, computers, faxes, and every form of modern communication to reopen the river, as they would have to contact each of the hundreds of companies and people to get business moving again. Captain Paskewich needed two very big plans, one to shut down the river for a hurricane and one to move his entire operation elsewhere if New Orleans was hit hard. Sometimes, the second plan, the Continuity of Operations Plan, which had never been used, is neglected in favor of more seemingly pressing emergency preparedness. Thankfully, Captain Paskewich decided to update a rather old and outdated plan in the early months of 2005.

Captain Paskewich had been assigned to New Orleans several times, serving both in the Marine Safety Office and in District Headquarters. He had married a local lady many years before, and his familiarity with the New Orleans area meant that he had a very good grasp of hurricanes in general and of what a major storm could mean for New Orleans in particular. The downside of this repeated assignment in the same area, known in the service as "homesteading," is that it will seriously hurt an officer's chance for promotion to the senior ranks of Commander and Captain. The Coast Guard usually wants a well-rounded officer, one who has had various assignments around different sections of both the country and the Coast Guard. This meant that Frank Paskewich had achieved the rank of Captain and Commander of the new Sector New Orleans despite serious odds, but Captain Paskewich was exactly the right guy, in the right place, at the right time in history.

In the spring of 2005, he assigned two of his more senior officers to revamp the Continuity of Operations Plan, Commander Greg Depinet and Lieutenant Commander Jimmy Duckworth. These two very different officers would end up being quite a team and played a major role in the eventual success the Coast Guard had in Katrina. Commander Depinet was a Coast Guard aviator assigned to the Marine Safety Office as the planning officer. He had flown for many years and then had left the Coast Guard to fly for commercial airlines. Unfortunately, his airline was bought out and downsized during an industry downturn. With airline hiring on hold, Depinet applied to and was allowed to come back into the Coast Guard, but there weren't any flying jobs available at the time and he was sent to MSO New Orleans. Jimmy Duckworth was a reserve officer recalled to active duty after the terrorist attacks of September 11, 2001. Duckworth was raised in New Orleans and owns a tire and repair shop in the New Orleans area. Being a reserve officer meant that normally he worked one weekend a month and two weeks a year. But like many reservists after 9/11, he was called back to active duty and was working full time for the Coast Guard. Interestingly Duckworth's background was in rescue boat operations at Coast Guard Station New Orleans; he was a Group guy from the start. But when he was recalled to active duty following 9/11, he was assigned to the Marine Safety Office in New Orleans, where he quickly became very well versed in the Marine Safety missions. This assignment gave Duckworth experience in the full range of Coast Guard missions ashore. And unusual for a Coast Guard officer, he had lived in the region all his life. He thus brought a tremendous amount of local knowledge to the assignment, something regular Coast Guard personnel, who transfer every three years or so, simply don't have.

So Depinet and Duckworth took the old Continuity of Operations Plan, or COOP as it was known, and got to work. With Duckworth's knowledge of both the area and the many missions of the Marine Safety Office, they updated the plan, making sure every aspect was current and workable in a disaster. Then they began looking for a place to relocate the Marine Safety Office headquarters in the event of a devastating hurricane. They needed a location with excellent communications, as the MSO staff would be contacting hundreds of companies and directing scores of vessels and various oil refineries, chemical plants, and shipping facilities along the river. They needed strong computer support and housing for all the displaced Coasties and their families, who would need a place to live in the aftermath of a mega-storm. And the place had to be close enough to New Orleans that the MSO crew could shut down the river before the storm and still have time to make it to the COOP location and set up operations before the hurricane hit. This was a very tough set of requirements, and the two officers traveled all over south Louisiana to scout potential locations.

Duckworth, with his Marine Safety Office experience and river background, liked Natchez, Mississippi. A beautiful town set on a bluff high above the river, Natchez is no longer the major river port it was in its glory days. There were office spaces available and hotel accommodations could be reserved on a contingency contract. But Depinet had his doubts, and they kept looking. Eventually they found Alexandria, a small town of about fifty thousand located in the exact center of the state, about four hours away from New Orleans and nowhere near the Mississippi River, but Depinet liked it a lot. Alexandria had the advantage, at least in his eyes, of having the former England Air Force Base, now closed and mostly quiet but with the runways still intact and in good repair.

When I arrived in New Orleans, the first thing I did was look at the hurricane plans. Having been previously assigned to Group Mobile, Alabama, I realized how important these plans were, and in late July, we were officially in hurricane season, with the peak of the season, normally August and September, right around the corner. In early July, Hurricane Cindy had passed through southern Louisiana, and sitting in my new and still empty house, my kids had thrilled to watch the pine trees bend way over. Early July is early for a hurricane to hit, and everybody sensed this could be a rough year. We had no idea that 2005 would be the most active hurricane year on record.

I looked at the Group hurricane plan first; it looked reasonable. Then I looked at the MSO plans, and while I approved of the hurricane plan, the COOP plan for moving the operations to a safe place didn't make much sense to me. Alexandria wasn't near any major city, was quite a distance from New Orleans, and was nowhere near the river.

My first question was, "Who picked Alexandria?" Captain Paskewich laughed and said to talk to Commander Depinet. I did. Depinet explained that the town had good internet and phone capabilities, was far enough from New Orleans to be safe from a storm that might incapacitate the city, and had a retired air force base we could use. I wasn't particularly impressed. I thought it was too far away and didn't much care about the runways on the old air base. But it was far too late to change the plan; a contingency contract had been let for use of the Alexandria Convention Center and another one for the Holiday Inn to house the Coasties and their families. And with the huge amount of staff work involved in combining the MSO and Group into the new Sector, everybody was far too busy to revamp a contingency plan anyway.

Events were to prove the tremendous wisdom of Commander Greg Depinet and Lieutenant Commander Jimmy Duckworth

The Convention Center in Alexandria, Louisiana, became the temporary Coast Guard Sector New Orleans Headquarters for the Katrina operation. (USCG)

for picking Alexandria and of Captain Paskewich for seeing the benefits this plan had to offer. As we got heavily into the rescue and recovery after Katrina, it became obvious to all that Alexandria offered tremendous benefits to every single aspect of our operation, often in very unexpected ways. Many believed the choice was truly inspired. Greg Depinet, as a fully qualified aviator, may have wondered why he was assigned to a Marine Safety Office, and Jimmy Duckworth may have wondered why he was still needed on active duty four years after 9/11, but it was soon obvious to me why both were on duty in New Orleans, at the MSO, just before Katrina. Thank God they were.

Creativity, Inc.

Lieutenant Alfred Jackson led his eighteen-member Disaster Assistance Response Team into the flooded city of New Orleans on Day Two. It was a busy time, and his job was to make things happen. As a lieutenant, Jackson was in his prime as a Coast Guard officer. He had been promoted twice to reach the rank of full Lieutenant and had survived the typical mistake-prone early years as a commissioned officer, obviously with success. He had significant authority yet was still young enough to connect easily with his crew of men and women mostly in their high teens and early twenties. It is well known that lieutenants are the backbone of the Coast Guard officer corps, and during Katrina, Lieutenant Jackson was to prove his worth over and over.

The Coast Guard was the nation's first permanent seagoing service, established by Congress in 1790 as the Revenue Cutter Service. When war later threatened with the Barbary Pirates and then France, Congress established a Navy as well. From the very beginning, the Cutters worked in close coordination with the Navy in times of war, providing the small and fast shallow water cutters to augment the Navy's powerful seagoing ships. In recent decades the Navy and Coast Guard have continued to work well together in both war and peace. The Navy deployed ships under Coast Guard command for counter-narcotics operations in the Caribbean and eastern Pacific. Coast Guard cutters served under Navy command in World War II, Vietnam, and both Iraq wars, and cutters continue to do work with the Navy when specialized Coast Guard capabilities are needed.

But a Navy is not a Coast Guard, nor vice versa. The Navy typically operates large and powerfully equipped ships in battle groups around the world, influencing friends and deterring enemies as needed. Navy ships are always ready to bring highly coordinated and intensely concentrated destruction on the nation's enemies when required. By contrast, the Coast Guard is a very small military service, with only about forty thousand active duty personnel in uniform, and they conduct a wide range of missions, including search and rescue, homeland security, fisheries protection, marine safety, pollution response and clean up, marine inspection, vessel traffic coordination, and ice breaking. The Coast Guard's mission set typically requires just one smaller ship, boat, helicopter, or airplane. In the case of marine inspection, often a single person is required to get the job done.

The nature of Coast Guard missions makes for a culture of highly motivated individual thinkers. The training of young Coasties is intense to ensure a high sense of team work and camaraderie as well as to instill standardized procedures for doing things as required in all five military services. But recognizing that they may be operating without support, they are also taught to adapt and overcome, to solve any problems they may encounter, and above all to get the job done. With such a small service spread all over the nation's coasts and waterways, and indeed all over the world for some missions, calling the boss for advice or directions isn't always an option, nor is it desired. Lieutenant Jackson would exemplify this culture in the days ahead when communications were spotty or nonexistent, and his creativity would save countless lives.

Just getting his team to New Orleans was an undertaking in itself. Coming down from St. Louis as the storm was passing through was quite an adventure. For great distances outside the city, roads were blocked by trees and power lines. With Interstate 10 washed away to the east and flooded to the west, they had to cross the damaged Causeway Bridge across Lake Pontchartrain. The rhythmic bumping on the old southbound span, a light and constant jolt for twenty-four miles, must have provided a background to the chorus of their worried thoughts. With no radio or television access, they would have had little idea of the devastation they would find. When they reached the southern end of the seemingly endless bridge, they were slowed by minor flooding right where the bridge exits into Jefferson Parish. The trucks and boat trailers made it through the standing water, but this was only a foreshadowing of what they would come to find. Lieutenant Jackson led his team to St. Claude Avenue, where they launched their boats into the flooded streets and went to work.

Jackson's DART team rescued more than two hundred people that first day of operations. It was hot and exhausting work, rescuing hundreds of people, one person at a time.

Downed trees were a serious problem for small boat operations on both dry land and water. (USCG, PA1 Bauman)

Each case was different; some rescues were easy, some were very difficult, and some seemed impossible. At the end of that first day of rescue, August 30, Lieutenant Jackson led his exhausted team to take shelter at the Naval Support Activity East Bank. This minimally manned Navy base provided a safe haven. Fortunately he reached the base before the crowds started to gather outside the gate. The next morning they had to resume rescue operations, but first they had to get through the angry and fraught survivors who had gathered during the night. Using tact and skill, they made it past the crowd at dawn and headed out.

The team began their day with some concerns. They had shared their limited supplies with those they rescued, and they were out of food and water from their efforts the previous day. Lieutenant Jackson, in a display of coordination, worked with the helicopters from Air Station New Orleans to resupply

Navigating through a flooded neighborhood. (USCG)

his crew so they could continue the effort to save as many people as quickly as possible. This was one of the first, but certainly not the last, time Coast Guard helicopters resupplied the small DART flood punts. Obviously the helicopters were engaged in a monumental rescue effort of their own, but it was vital for the boat crews in those early days that the helicopters would leave their airfield at Belle Chasse loaded with food and water, drop them off for the DART teams, then proceed with their own rescue hoist operations. Though aviators and boat guys often give each other a hard time in friendly rivalry, they work together day in and day out throughout the Coast Guard in highly coordinated operations, and each appreciates that the other will be there when needed.

Now resupplied, Lieutenant Jackson and his crew continued their rescue operations. Help was starting to arrive. The Federal Emergency Management Agency and the Coast Guard set up a unified command at Zephyr Field baseball park, known to us as the summer practice field of the New Orleans Saints. Initially Coast Guard boat crews from the now-flooded Integrated Support Command were among the first Coasties to work with the FEMA crews, and it was clear that coordinated operations were the best way to go. This operation, called Urban Search and Rescue (USAR), combined Coast Guard and FEMA rescue boats. The FEMA boats were manned mostly by firemen and law enforcement volunteers brought into the city by FEMA, and they did an amazing job, rescuing thousands of stranded people. As the operation grew in numbers of FEMA and Coast Guard boats, the coordination efforts of the USAR team at Zephyr Field became increasingly important. By September 2, there were 16 Coast Guard boats and 65 Coasties working on the USAR team. Only twenty-four hours later the numbers had doubled to 30 boats and 120 Coasties. The USAR staff developed and maintained a highly specialized grid system covering the city and accounting for the winding river and various canals, rail lines, major streets, and neighborhoods. This unorthodox but highly effective grid was adopted by the Army and other military services when they were finally allowed to commence operations. The USAR staff directed the daily searches to ensure every flooded neighborhood was searched three times by boat. This was done to ensure none were missed and every single person could be rescued. It was an amazing operation, and initially Lieutenant Commander Daryl Schaffer helped set it up, working frantically in those first hectic days. As the operation quickly grew, it became imperative to assign a semi-permanent staff so they could make the best use of their rapidly increasing numbers of boats and crews. Lieutenant Commander Shannon Gilreath, a man very well versed in all Coast Guard operations, was sent down with two officers and proved highly skilled in unified operations. Much of the Coast Guard success in the surface rescue operation is due to the efforts of Gilreath and his work at USAR.

Even though coordinated operations had begun, on the water things were increasingly difficult. On Day Three, Lieutenant Jackson and his boats ran into some New Orleans correctional officers needing assistance. The Coasties then came under sniper fire, and Lieutenant Jackson quickly led his boats and the correctional officers out of the line of fire. This was a growing problem, as criminals continued to roam the area looking for victims, and law-abiding citizens were frightened and quickly learning to shoot in self-defense, often without determining exactly at whom they were shooting.

With the criminal element firmly in mind, Lieutenant Jackson was looking to protect his rescue boats. With only six weapons and eight sets of body armor to protect his now larger team of sixty-five personnel, Jackson devised the "security boat" concept wherein one Coastie, armed and fully protected by body armor, made sure he was quite visible and intimidating, while several other boats conducted rescues in that immediate area. It worked for three more days until more weapons and body armor could be delivered. Later, Coast Guard Maritime Safety and Security Teams arrived to take over the protection of

Lieutenant Commander Shannon Gilreath holds a briefing at Zephyr Field, headquarters for the joint Coast Guard/FEMA Unified Command which ultimately rescued more than twelve thousand people in the little flood punts. (USCG)

the little boats. Later still the Army's 82nd Airborne Division would arrive and take on some of this protection. In both cases, the security boat tactics developed by Lieutenant Jackson served as the foundation for all USAR teams.

Working with USAR, Jackson heard of several thousand people stranded and desperate in the Chalmette and St. Bernard areas. Many of these people were truly in a difficult situation. Not only had their city and parish flooded severely, in some places as much as twenty feet deep, but massive oil storage tanks at the local refinery, Murphy Oil, were breached by the massive flood. These ruptured tanks released as much as a million gallons of oil, along with the very dangerous hydrogen sulfide gas that accompanies any significant oil spill. The toxins were spreading throughout the flooded community. It was truly an unbelievable and very dangerous mess. Making the situation worse, rescue boats couldn't reach Chalmette or St. Bernard Parish due to the distance from their Zephyr Field base, and the vessels couldn't be trailered there because of the flooding of critical roads. Jackson had the idea of fitting the small flood punts into the Army heavy-lift helicopters that were operating at the base. The boats, stacked on their trailers, just barely fit into the helicopters. The helicopters would fly the boats and their crews out first thing in the morning, the boats would rescue people from this natural and man-made disaster all day, and the helicopters would return in the evening and pick up the same boats, their crews, and the rescued people. It was an excellent example of inter-service coordination and creative thinking.

Later Lieutenant Jackson coordinated one of the most dramatic rescues conducted by Coastie small boats. Seven days after the storm, his team located an eighty-seven-year-old woman and her son trapped on the second floor of their house with water up to their chests. Doctors had predicted several days earlier that survival in the intense heat was increasingly unlikely, especially for the ill and elderly. On that day, the boats were driving down the flooded street doing a search when a coxswain felt something amiss. The engines were shut off so that the crews could listen, and in this case he felt pulled to look closely at one particular house. As they drove closer, they heard a faint tapping coming from a barred second-story window. The boat crews had to use chainsaws to cut through the roof and the ceiling of the house. Complicating things further, the elderly lady was bedridden and most of her body had been submerged beneath the flood waters for the last seven days. Her immersion in the polluted waters had wrought havoc on her body and her skin. She was in critical condition and required special care while moving her out of the house so she wouldn't damage more of her skin. Both mother and son were safely evacuated from the house and were then medevacked so she could receive

Coasties loading flood punts into an Army CH-47 helicopter. This air mobility was essential for rescue operations in and around Chalmette, as that badly flooded area couldn't be reached any other way. The helicopters would transport boats and crews from Zephyr Field in the morning to Chalmette, where the boat crews would conduct rescues all day. In the evening, the helicopters would return, load the boats, along with the crews and those they had rescued, and return them to Zephyr Field. (USCG)

immediate medical attention. Some of the boat crews thought such a survival and rescue story was impossible, and one Coastie said he couldn't understand at first why they felt drawn to that particular house. But the old woman was a woman of intense faith, and her prayers had been answered. It was reported to me that when the Coasties showed up, she said, "I knew if I waited here long enough, you boys would come get me. Thank you, Lord!"

I Hate It When the
Pilot Says That

Everyone at both Marine Safety Office New Orleans and Group New Orleans had worked very hard to combine the two units into Sector New Orleans. Each unit had a full captain as its commanding officer, reflecting the importance and great responsibility of each command. Both had full staffs of personnel dedicated to their individual operations, and both had long experience in their respective missions. To combine them and then divide up the new responsibilities between the combined staffs was a challenge, as was moving the senior staff of the Marine Safety Office into the former Group headquarters on Lake Pontchartrain. To avoid the intense heat of New Orleans in August, the Change of Command Ceremony was to be held at 9:30 in the morning on August 18. But even the ceremony, always a very traditional and quite formal military ceremony complete with swords and white gloves, had to be altered to fit the new circumstances. As they taught back at the Academy, trained initiative and leadership can accomplish anything, and so it was that the combined Sector New Orleans Commissioning Ceremony, the Change of Command Ceremony, and a retirement ceremony were all held as a single event, on time, on schedule, fairly early that August morning.

After the big ceremony, a few more days were spent getting things squared away; new personnel settled into their now rather crowded offices and new duties were assigned to all. Everyone was tired and looking forward to a party, the first Sector party with all hands from both previous units, on Friday evening, August 26. We had heard of this new hurricane, Katrina, and in fact had tracked it as it turned into a hurricane near the Bahamas, forming from a new tropical wave and the remnants of a tropical depression. We watched it tear a path of destruction across south Florida and emerge into the Gulf. The Coast Guard follows all hurricanes, and as this one grew stronger and stronger, we watched it with great interest. But clearly it was headed for the western Florida panhandle and would probably make its second landfall near Destin or Pensacola. While we felt sorry for the unfortunates in its path, we were all pretty tired and thankful it wasn't headed toward us. I even called my parents, who were living in Destin, Florida, and advised them to get out of there before Katrina hit and to come stay with me in Mandeville, just north of New Orleans, where it was safe. My father said they would ride this one out at home. I worried about them, but it turned out they were quite safe after all.

Friday evening finally rolled around and we are all having a nice, relaxing party in a little outdoor park near Lake Pontchartrain. Burgers and dogs are on the grill; sodas and water are in the coolers. The officers and enlisted personnel from the two commands are getting to know each other in a more relaxed environment, and everyone is having a good time, eating good food, enjoying new friends, and often telling "sea stories." Frank and I are talking, some about our days together back at the Academy, some about the new Sector we were building, some about that hurricane fixing to hit Florida. Then a junior officer approached us: "Sir, it's not turning as expected; Katrina is coming here." We asked if he was sure. The storm had been tracking west and was supposed to take the normal curve to the north and hit Florida, but Katrina was getting so big that it seemed to be making its own steering currents. It was now headed for the northern Gulf Coast, with New Orleans in its crosshairs.

Frank and I looked at each other, our minds racing. We had a very large storm heading straight for us, a strong Category 3 and building fast. It was anticipated that it would hit early Monday morning, which meant its expected landfall was already inside not only our 96-hour planning deadline but also our 72-hour planning deadline. We were already two days behind on the hurricane plan for shutting down the port. While the compressed timeline was a disadvantage for the small boat stations, patrol boats, and aids to navigation teams, it was a disaster in the making for the Marine Safety mission. To close down the port in 48 hours seemed impossible.

We decided that since our combined staffs were so new to their positions, we would work along the missions our people knew. Frank would take the Marine Safety mission with some bleed over for Boat Operations, and I would take Boat Operations with some bleed over into Marine Safety, and we went to work. Frank set the former Marine Safety experts to making the calls and doing the inspections necessary to facilitate the closing of the port. I got busy with the former Group staff and we prepared the stations, patrol boats, and Aids to Navigation Teams to fuel up, stock up, crew up, evacuate, and then be ready for operations as soon as the storm passed.

Frank called a staff meeting early the next morning, Saturday, as the city woke up to the potential disaster heading its way. All Sector personnel, both in the port with the commercial operations and with the various Coast Guard rescue units, had been busy all night making the calls and arrangements needed to face the Category 3 storm heading our way. All department heads made their reports, and given the timeline, the discussions were relatively compressed.

Things were going well, considering the very short time we had before the storm. Even though we were now only about 44 hours out from the first hurricane-force winds hitting the city, and thus about 30 hours out from the first of the hurricane's winds hitting Southwest Pass at the mouth of the Mississippi River and Station Grand Isle, we were quickly crossing off items on the 96-, 72-, and 48-hour checklists. Everybody in the New Orleans area was very aware that a massive storm was headed straight for the city, and the entire marine industry was extremely responsive to all Coast Guard requests and orders. It was well understood how vulnerable the port was and that to ensure the safety of both ships and people, facilities along the river had to follow the Coast Guard's directives. It was amazing to me how cooperative and congenial the maritime world was in New Orleans, something I had not seen in any other port where I had been stationed.

The small boat side was going very well too. All station, patrol boat, and aids to navigation crews were working at flank speed to get things secured and all vessels out of the projected path of the storm. In shipboard terms, full speed is the maximum speed that can be sustained for any length of time. Flank speed is like an emergency sprint, beyond full speed. That was to become our normal operations tempo, or "op tempo," for the next few weeks. Because Katrina was already a massive storm, and getting bigger by the hour, I decided to send the small boats on trailers in all different directions to seek shelter. This wasn't part of the established plan, but I felt strongly led to scatter them across eastern Louisiana and western Mississippi. My thought was that even if some were hit by the storm, if the boats were widely separated, some would survive. As it turned out, all of the boats made it through Katrina just fine, and being spread out, all crews were able to start rescues or major assistance where they were sheltering. As a result, even more lives were saved in those critical first two days.

This is the way it was for me more often than not during the Katrina rescue and recovery. I would be led to make an intuitive decision that I could only explain on a simple level. But as things unfolded, the results would prove far better than I could have ever expected. As the storm approached, I was praying hard but rather quickly. I was very well aware of the magnitude of the storm and that decisions had to be right or the consequences could be serious. I asked the Lord to show me what to do. I wasn't aware of his leadership. I didn't hear his voice, and yet, looking back, it is clear that he was guiding me all along.

The next order of business was implementing the Continuity of Operations Plan (COOP), a new plan never before used. By Sunday morning Katrina had become a Category 4 storm and was expected to reach Category 5 strength, the highest category on the Saffir-Simpson Hurricane Wind Scale. Beyond the amazing wind strength and high storm surge, the storm itself was massive in scale. The satellite photos we were seeing looked like the weather system would seriously impact areas as far east as Florida and as far west as Texas and absolutely hammer New Orleans. Frank, having lived in New Orleans for years and understanding only too well the vulnerability of the low-lying parts of the city to flooding, ordered the plan into effect. We were getting out of Dodge, all of us.

Frank and his former MSO staff were working at flank speed to shut down the five ports in the New Orleans area. In the midst of this operation, he would be taking about half of his staff up to Alexandria to establish a new Sector headquarters in the convention center there, as per the COOP plan. Many would be making important phone calls as they drove through the congestion of the evacuating traffic. I would stay in New Orleans with the rest of the staff to see to the evacuation of the rescue units and the final closures of the river, this last under the close supervision of the Marine Safety professionals. Embedded into all of this was getting our families packed and out of the city as well, most headed to Alexandria. I had never seen so many people move so fast and with such sense of purpose. To close down one of the largest port complexes in the world on such a compressed timeline while shifting headquarters to an unprepared location and simultaneously moving families during a five- or six-hour drive was truly a monumental event.

On the river, things were moving just as quickly. While we may have had forty-four hours' notice in New Orleans before the storm hit, for the huge ships visiting the ports, the timeline was much shorter. The entrance for large ships into the Mississippi River is Southwest Pass, some eighty miles southeast of the city. At Southwest Pass, there would only be twenty-four hours until large waves in the area made the river pilots' task of getting on and off the ships, transferring from a small pilot boat to the large ship by climbing up the rope Jacob's ladder, far too dangerous. Without a river pilot, a large ship simply can't transit the Mississippi River. This river turns and twists, has a narrow channel that deep-draft ships must stay inside, and has sandbars that constantly shift with currents and the river stage. Maneuvering a large ship through this river is very difficult in the best of times, and every move requires forethought and planning.

For example, to turn the ship to the right, a pilot must order the helmsman to turn the rudder to the right and then wait ten or twenty seconds or longer before the ship starts to change course. The pilot must then order the rudder shifted back and wait another ten to twenty seconds before the ship stops turning. Speeding up or slowing down a large ship can take even longer as a heavy ship has tremendous momentum to overcome, and there are no brakes. To stop a large ship can take well over a mile.

When you put such a vessel on a twisting and turning river with a narrow channel barely deep enough to hold the ship, you must have a pilot onboard who knows the river like the back of his hand and knows exactly how to drive an eight-hundred-foot ship in such a challenging place. With the waves of Katrina building rapidly, the timeline to get the pilots on and off and the big ships out of the river was very short.

During a hurricane, large ships need to be in the open ocean, hopefully steaming toward the western side of the storm, the safe side, where the winds are a little weaker and the waves are quite a bit smaller. If they can't make the open ocean, large ships need to be securely anchored in the river with additional shots of heavy chain out and a second anchor set deep. Ships can't be at a dock during a hurricane, as the resulting waves and rising river levels will hammer a ship against the dock, destroying both. If the ship were a tanker and the dock were an oil refinery, the consequences could be catastrophic. Thus the Coast Guard's immediate goal was to get the ships underway that were capable of leaving before the pilots had to close Southwest Pass. Failing that, the ships remaining in the river needed to be anchored securely in the designated anchorages. This is not as easy as it sounds. There are always more ships at dock and in transit than spots in the anchorages. So diverting incoming ships away from New Orleans to other ports and getting ships already in the river out to sea when possible were critical.

Shutting down and properly securing the various shipping facilities, docks, and other services on the river was also a priority. The oil refineries, chemical plants, and industry on the river had to be shut down too, boarded up so to speak, and made ready for rising water on the river as well as 150 mile-per-hour winds. With a large plant employing several thousand people, it was quite a task, and there a number of such plants along the stretch of the lower Mississippi River.

Smaller vessels need to be stowed on trailers far inland or, if floating, hidden in "hurricane holes," tied securely by many lines and protected by land from strong waves. Think of a hurricane hole as a cul-de-sac on the water, surrounded by land on almost all sides, providing protection from the wind and waters. On the lower Mississippi River, there is only one good hurricane hole, at Chalmette Slip, and it fills up fast with towboats, crew boats, fishing boats, and even a floating grain elevator. The slip was packed so tightly, you could walk from one side to the other, from vessel to vessel, and not get your feet wet. But the small Coast Guard rescue boats needed to get far from the city. The 41-footers and 55-footers went up in a small convoy to Baton Rouge. While Baton Rouge isn't exactly a hurricane hole, it is well west of New Orleans, and we thought it was far enough away to escape the most serious winds of the storm. The trailered boats were loaded up and sent to various shelter areas throughout eastern Louisiana and western Mississippi, with excellent results as it turned out, both in protecting the boats and in making immediate rescues near the areas they had gone for shelter. The 87-foot patrol boats were sent west to Texas, this being the "safe" side of the hurricane, such as it was, and thus even if the storm ended up tracking west, the patrol boats would be on the side of the lesser winds and waves. Should the storm head straight for Houston, we could shift the patrol boats even farther west and south along the Texas and even Mexican coast as needed and keep them safe.

As I oversaw the final preparations from New Orleans, Captain Frank Paskewich and the advance team arrived in Alexandria fairly quickly, it only being about a four- or five-hour drive that Saturday since most of the city had not started to evacuate yet. It would be a much longer trip for the second half of the staff leaving on Sunday after closing down the port. Frank's team worked out the reservations with the hotel, set up the computers and phone lines, arranged the work spaces, and procured food sources. While the advance team was setting up the basics, they were also establishing the ICS, or Incident Command Structure, that we would use to run all hurricane and recovery operations. This system, first used by firefighters in the west, was designed to let people from many different backgrounds work together in a common framework, and it can quickly be expanded as the situation dictates. Our situation would dictate rapid and repeated expansion.

Still in New Orleans, I was with the remaining Sector staff. We had teams coordinating bridge closures, oil facility shut-downs, and a large number of extra safety precautions across all river industries and facilities to account for the unprecedented severity of this storm, which was now almost a Category Five. At the four rescue stations, they were locking things down, closing storm doors and shutters, and making everything as secure as they could against this monster storm before the boat crews evacuated with the boats to safety.

Across the city, residents were doing the same for their own homes before they would join the mass exodus from New Orleans. Members of the second team departed the New Orleans area on Sunday afternoon. Unfortunately, it seemed most of the city was also leaving Sunday afternoon, headed for points north, and traffic was a nightmare. What should have been a four-hour trip to Alexandria now took nine or ten hours. At least the Coasties knew where they were headed; many of the rest of the evacuees from the city did not.

Some of these refugees had reservations at hotels, but the rooms along the major evacuation routes quickly filled up. Many people just drove north and hoped to find accommodations somewhere along the way, far enough away from New Orleans to be safe from Katrina's worst. This proved to be more difficult than many expected, as Katrina spawned tornadoes that wreaked havoc across the Gulf Coast. Coast Guard families that evacuated to Naval Air Station Meridian, Mississippi, about two hundred miles north of New Orleans, were hit with a series of tornadoes that snapped the tall pine trees like twigs, blocking all roads, and shutting down the power system for several days. But being so far inland, they were spared the flooding. Unfortunately though, those near the coast in Louisiana, Mississippi, Alabama, and even as far away as Pensacola, Florida, did have flooding from the huge storm surge that Katrina produced and the devastation such flooding always brings.

When we finally arrived in Alexandria, I was deeply impressed by what the advance team had accomplished. The hotel check-in was easy and the new command center was up and running smoothly with a skeleton staff, one that the second team soon fleshed out. Clearly this was going to be a 24-7 event, so we quickly divided into watches—two twelve-hour shifts, a day watch and a night watch—to work twenty-four hours a day, seven days a week, until the crisis was over. Frank and I would co-lead the day watch. I would run the rescue operations and Frank would run the Marine Safety operations on the river and elsewhere as needed. It turned out there were many "elsewheres" for the Marine Safety team.

The offshore oil facilities were initially a major concern for Captain Paskewich. Although that field was busy, it wasn't the disaster it easily could have been. Most of the oil facilities off the Louisiana coast and into the Gulf of Mexico south of Louisiana were in Frank's area of responsibility as the Sector New Orleans Commander. However, because the Mississippi River is such a major focus and is an overriding concern for the Sector staff, there is a sub-unit of Sector, Marine Safety Unit Morgan City, or MSU Morgan City, that holds the primary responsibility for much of the Louisiana offshore oil facilities. The Louisiana offshore is so important that MSU Morgan City also has a full Captain in charge, in this case Captain Terry Gilbreath.

Captain Gilbreath and his team had done a masterful job of working with the industry to evacuate the hundreds of rigs and facilities that make up the Louisiana oil patch. With thousands of men working offshore, this was no easy task, yet it was done rapidly and efficiently. In addition to evacuations, the oil wells and undersea pipelines had to be shut down so that if a rig or platform were damaged, no oil would leak. It was feared that oil spills would be a huge issue with so powerful a storm hitting the vulnerable Louisiana oil coast, and while many rigs were damaged and a couple sank, there were no significant oil spills offshore. The press did report some suspected discharges, but when Coast Guard crew flew aircraft to investigate, there was nothing to be found other than a couple of very light sheens, the kind we often see in the Gulf due to natural seepage from the marine floor. That alone seems to qualify as another minor miracle; the possibility for disaster was certainly very high.

Having shut down the oil field, Captain Gilbreath and

his Morgan City crew were also arriving in Alexandria as planned. This crew of Marine Safety experts was to prove as invaluable in running the new command center as Terry would be to our leadership team. With the oil field shut down, freeing him from the responsibilities of his usual command, Terry took over the night watch in the command center, allowing Frank and I to work together on the day shift. The night watch was critically important, gathering the results of that day's operations throughout southern Louisiana and Mississippi, chasing down and ordering the supplies, boats, and people needed to fill identified requirements, and setting up operations for the next day. It is said in military circles that "amateurs focus on tactics; generals focus on logistics," and this was certainly true in the rescue and recovery operations in the aftermath of Katrina.

It was a late night for us all that Sunday evening, and with Katrina reaching Category 5 strength earlier that afternoon, everyone was wound up and completing their final tasks at full speed. The watches were split up, and the day shift went to catch some sleep before Katrina hit the next morning. Sleep was hard for many, as emotions were running high.

While the day watch rested, the night watch remained busy setting up the new command center, reaching out and checking on all the smaller Coast Guard units scattered across southern Louisiana and Mississippi, coordinating with industry, and working with the other governmental agencies that were setting up command centers of their own.

The Incident Command Structure, the ICS that we were using, is made up of four main elements: the ICS commander, the operations department, the logistics department, and the planning department. We used this system twenty-four hours a day, with two shifts. Frank and I shared the job of ICS commander during the day those first few days, as each of our missions was a full-time job and each needed the complete attention of a Captain, particularly as we were dealing with so many other military units. In the military,

Captain Frank Paskewich and I, wearing command vests, setting up the command center at the Alexandria convention center on the Sunday night before Katrina hit. We are flanked by Commander Scott Paradis, Lieutenant Commander Greg Purvis, and Commander Jim Whitehead as we gather to discuss a myriad of details. We were using the Incident Command Structure developed by firefighters to handle massive fires out west. The ICS allows for a rapidly expanding disaster while maintaining good command and control of events. Given what we expected from Katrina, it was a perfect system for what we needed. (USCG)

rank counts when things need to get done. With a reduced operational workload at night, Captain Terry Gilbreath held the ISC command at night. Ops, logistics and planning were all very busy that Sunday evening. Nobody knew exactly what we would face the next day but all wanted to be ready for whatever came. The Coast Guard motto *Semper Paratus,* "Always Ready," was in full force that night. At last we reached the point where everything that could be done was done.

The next morning was busy, but anticlimactic. The storm had hit and we were receiving a few reports, but the Coast

Guard boat crews, teams, and the remaining population of the city were hunkered down as the storm passed. We stayed very busy working with our liaison officers assigned to other agencies, as everybody was setting up lines of communication and establishing procedures for what was surely to be an operation on a scale that none of us had ever experienced. As the morning progressed, reports came in of tremendous wind damage and trees and power lines down throughout the region. Even though the winds of Katrina had weakened a little by the time the storm hit and were downgraded to a strong Category 3, the damage was still incredible. But the television told a different story, at least at first. We were watching both CNN and Fox News, and these networks were broadcasting scenes from the French Quarter of people and buildings emerging relatively unscathed. Despite the positive images on the television, we began to receive reports of serious flooding, and not just along the coast where we expected it.

We knew coastal communities would experience devastating flooding from the storm surge. While the winds of Katrina may have slackened, the wall of water ahead of it had continued to build, and it reached massive proportions, unknown in modern history. After the storm, damage to the few remaining buildings in the Gulfport, Mississippi, area indicated the storm surge was something like thirty to thirty-five feet high. It wasn't quite the towering wave of water that we see in the movies. It was a relentless force that keeps building and coming and destroying and washing away everything in its path. The destruction from such rushing water can be nearly total, and in many places it was. We also expected severe flooding along the north shore of Lake Pontchartrain, where the massive surge of ocean water pushed into the lake rose higher and higher until it consumed parts of Slidell, Mandeville, and Madisonville. What we were not expecting was to hear of flooding within New Orleans itself.

Confirming anything was very difficult while Katrina raged, but by early afternoon the small orange HH-65 helicopters

HH-60J Jayhawk, the type of helicopter Captain Paskewich and I flew on that first disaster assessment flight over the flooded city. (USCG)

from Station New Orleans were coming around behind the storm to enter the city and make a first assessment. It turns out they would be making rescues and hoisting survivors from the very start. We also had some of the larger HH-60s available from Coast Guard Air Station Mobile, Alabama, and Frank and I took off in one of these Monday afternoon for our initial assessment of the damage and to determine what would be required in the days ahead. This was our first use of the runway that Commander Greg Depinet had deemed essential when selecting Alexandria as the COOP site. We would soon call it Air Station Alexandria, as the old England Air Force Base became a hub of Coast Guard aviation activity.

As we flew from Alexandria to New Orleans, conditions gradually grew worse and worse the closer we came to the city. We flew over our 41-footers and 55-footers making their way downriver from Baton Rouge, slowly heading back to New Orleans. From the air we could see how difficult their progress would be with trash and large debris all over the river and along the riverbanks. Our thin-skinned boats had to be careful not to hit anything that could punch a hole in a hull or destroy a propeller. Either would end the mission for that boat and crew immediately. The crews were very conscious of the need to get their boats undamaged to New Orleans, ready for operations, so they could help with the rescue.

Closer to the city, the signs of destruction increased rapidly. As we flew east-southeast towards New Orleans, we saw with surprise that Interstate I-10 west of New Orleans, the main highway in and out of the city, was now underwater and impassable. As we flew over Metairie in Jefferson Parish, the huge suburb adjoining the western side of New Orleans, we saw heavy damage: trees and power lines were down everywhere, roofs had been ripped off buildings, and, most ominous, many of the major roads were blocked by debris. But as of yet we saw no flooding in the city itself.

We were directed to fly to the Superdome to pick up a high-ranking official for the Federal Emergency Management Agency, Mr. Marty Bahomonde, and take him on a survey flight so he could report the damage to FEMA director Michael Brown. As Frank and I flew into the heart of the city from the west, we saw our first signs of flooding, though it didn't look too bad at first. I noted some flooding at the foot of the Causeway Bridge, where the spans made landfall on the south shore of Lake Pontchartrain. The floodwaters didn't look too deep at that location, but estimating water depth was very difficult from a helicopter.

We headed toward the lakefront Station New Orleans, where floodwaters were receding. It was obvious there had been serious flooding along the shoreline, as there was a huge pile of debris accumulated on the levee. The station building appeared to be intact, but we saw people gathering around the station, some of whom appeared to be trying to break into the building.

FEMA representative Marty Bahomonde and Captain Frank Paskewich on our first flight over the flooded city. The Coast Guard public affairs team gave me a camera before we took off and asked that I take a lot of photographs. Many of these photos of the flood rapidly overtaking New Orleans were from that first flight as Frank and I surveyed the damage and began to formulate our rescue and recovery plans, his for the river operations and mine for the upcoming rescue operations. (USCG, Captain Robert Mueller)

Nearby, the Southern Yacht Club, a yachting icon on the Gulf Coast, was both underwater and on fire. Its members were quite proud of being the second-oldest yacht club in America, only slightly younger than the New York Yacht Club. Before Katrina, the Southern Yacht Club was quite the place. As a new Captain in town, I previously had been issued an invitation for lunch on Tuesday, August 30, the day after Katrina hit. As I looked down on the building, the first floor underwater and the top of the building burning furiously from a broken gas line, I looked at Frank and said, "I don't think I'm going to make lunch tomorrow." He said somberly, "Probably not." Unfortunately the Yacht Club became emblematic of what we would see all over New Orleans.

As we flew over Lakeview, we could see the 17th Street

Canal had broken on the east side and was pouring huge amounts of water into that unfortunate neighborhood. Our pilot wanted to cut the assessment short and immediately start hoisting survivors from rooftops. Frank and I wanted to do so as well, but we had to keep going. A full assessment of the magnitude of the disaster that was now New Orleans would help us plan the entire rescue operation and that was critical in saving as many as possible. Before leaving Alexandria, we had initiated as many rescue operations as we could based on the information we had. While we were in the air, other Air Station New Orleans helicopters were already conducting rescue hoist operations, the DART boat

Our view of the 17th Street Canal Levee breech, flooding the Lakeview neighborhood. At this point Monday afternoon, water still flowed under Coast Guard Station New Orleans. The building on fire is the famous Southern Yacht Club, the ground floor underwater and the top floors on fire, a common sight in New Orleans as gas lines burst. (USCG, Captain Robert Mueller)

teams were en route to the flooded city, the Integrated Support Command and the Marine Safety Unit Baton Rouge boats were approaching New Orleans, and the various station boat crews were hacking their way back to the lake and other bodies of water to launch their boats.

We picked up Mr. Bahomonde at the Superdome and headed out for our survey. At that point, the Central Business District around the Superdome had wind damage but little water. As we headed east, Gentilly, the Bywater, and Treme, as well as the Lower Ninth Ward and parts of the Upper Ninth Ward, were all badly flooded, mostly from breaks in the levee along the Industrial Canal. The Industrial Canal runs between Lake Pontchartrain and the Mississippi River and was particularly vulnerable to the floods of Katrina. To the north, rising lake levels forced water back through the Industrial Canal, to be met by water rushing in from the MRGO canal (Mississippi River Gulf Outlet). The MRGO connected New Orleans with a direct shipping route to the Gulf of Mexico, via Lake Borgne, bypassing much of the river passage south. Unfortunately it also provided a direct route from the Gulf to New Orleans for the storm surge from Katrina. Under such pressure, the levees on the Industrial Canal didn't have a chance of holding. Flying over the Industrial Canal, we saw the break in the levee and witnessed the water rushing like river rapids into the Lower Ninth Ward. Such was the power of the water that houses were shoved off their foundations and floated away, and a 195-foot barge was sucked through the break in the levee, to become part of the devastation of the neighborhood.

Chalmette, a city abutting New Orleans to the east, was inundated, as were the towns and communities of Arabi, Meraux, Violet, and Poydras, all running down the east bank of the Mississippi River. These cities and towns were flooded by water overtopping the backside levees, which couldn't hope to hold back what was later estimated to be a twenty-five-foot storm surge. To the north, New Orleans East was also completely overwhelmed by water. The Home Depot was underwater and I thought about the supplies in that store that were now unavailable to those who would need them. Every store in that community was submerged, as were the car dealerships, their thousands of new cars now submarines, ruined forever. In neighborhoods roofs peaked out of the muddy waters like islands. People were starting to gather on

Interstate 610 crossing Elysian Fields, a major artery in the eastern part of the city. Years later, I drive this interstate and take this exit on my way to work every day. The recovery in New Orleans has been nothing short of amazing, though it is rarely reported in the media. (USCG, Captain Robert Mueller)

some of those rooftops. Above it all the roller coaster and other tall rides of the shuttered Six Flags New Orleans amusement park stood sentinel, the lower parts of the park hidden by fifteen feet of floodwater.

Having seen so much devastation, I was worried about how we were going to get rescue resources into the city, and I directed the pilot to fly east to look at Interstate 10 feeding into New Orleans from the east. What we saw was shocking. The massive four-lane I-10 Twin Span bridge was missing many of its huge concrete sections. The all-powerful storm surge coming into the lake through the Rigolets, a narrow passage between the Gulf of Mexico and Lake Pontchartrain, had just washed them away like they were made of sand. Interstate 10 was now useless, and unless the Causeway Bridge still stood, it looked like New Orleans was cut off completely by the flood.

Our first images of the flooded city, I-10 at Orleans Avenue, during our helicopter ride to survey the storm damage. (USCG, Captain Robert Mueller)

Obviously the next order of business was to fly the length of the twenty-four-mile-long Causeway Bridge in the middle of Lake Pontchartrain to determine whether it was still sound. The bridge was standing, but we couldn't tell from the air if it was useable for vehicles. After seeing the damage to the Twin Spans, we were concerned the Causeway's concrete deck might have shifted up or down in ways we couldn't see from the air but would stop a vehicle cold. Our concern was amplified when we noticed that the huge concrete turn-arounds underneath the main deck of the bridge had been washed away. These turn-arounds had been built in 1956 as part of the original two-lane bridge. They weren't used anymore as a second parallel bridge had been built in 1969 to provide two lanes in each direction. The destruction of the turn-arounds was not a good sign.

As we flew back over the city, we saw a large ship had been washed onto the river levee. Several tugboats were working to pull it back into deep water. The flood surge that raced up the river had pushed it and several other barges and towboats ashore. Debris of every kind was scattered around the port and the river itself. We dropped off Mr. Bahomonde at the Superdome to make his report, and we headed west, out of New Orleans.

It was a very somber flight back. Much of the city was underwater and the situation was clearly degenerating. Buildings were on fire, people needed rescue, and the main highway into and out of the city was impassable in both directions. Frank and I headed back with an overwhelming sense of the disaster we faced, and our minds were racing with all that we had to do.

As it was getting dark, the pilot had to divert to Lafayette to refuel before taking us back to Alexandria. We flew along in silence for a while, each alone with a thousand thoughts, until one of the pilots muttered, "Oh shit" over the intercom. I looked at Frank and said, "I hate it when the pilot says that." He laughed and said, "Me too." We gave the pilot a few minutes to sort things out and then asked what happened. He sheepishly said he had miscalculated the fuel; we might not make it to Lafayette. Looking down, there was not a light to be seen for miles in any direction, total blackout due to massive power failures. It could put a dent in the rescue and recovery operation if both of us died in a helicopter crash, but others would take the lead. It was now quiet over the intercom as we flew to Lafayette, a very long, tense twenty minutes. With the runway in site, we breathed a sigh of relief. We safely touched down and the engines died as we taxied to the refueling station. Thank you, Lord! I felt very blessed indeed.

Everything Is Biblical Proportions!

After refueling in Lafayette, we landed back in Alexandria with an understanding of the catastrophe we were facing and the scope of the recovery mission. Frank now had a good idea of the condition of the port and soon briefed the staff on what needed to be done. My focus was on the rapidly expanding rescue operation. Frank led the efforts in oil pollution, the offshore oil industry survey and response, and waterways restoration. Katrina had done quite a job. The river was full of debris and who knew how many sunken vessels and equipment. Offshore, several platforms were sunk and at least one major drilling rig was in serious trouble. Getting a count on the rest was very difficult since all were evacuated. This would be an incredibly complex operation on an unprecedented scale. So far the Sector had overseen an immediate shutdown of a major port complex, followed by the most destructive hurricane in history. Now the Sector crews had to clear the river of debris, set up the navigation aids, make the various facilities along the river safe, help the river pilots return to operation, and ultimately get shipping and commerce moving again, all while supporting the boat operations crews in the largest domestic search and rescue operation in history. It was a daunting task, but one the Marine Safety experts on staff were working on at a furious pace.

Key to the Coast Guard post-Katrina operations was the co-ordination between various government and industry leaders. In the next couple of days, many of the civilian leaders in the marine industry would relocate to Alexandria, and this greatly facilitated federal, state, and local efforts to reopen the river.

By relocating senior industry partners to Alexandria, communications were greatly simplified, and the process went far smoother and faster than anybody had a right to expect. This was another example of the wisdom of choosing Alexandria as the COOP site. While Baton Rouge was certainly much closer to New Orleans, was located on the river, and suffered only minor to moderate damage from the storm, every other federal, state, and local agency relocated there. In addition to the government folks, many industries had also relocated there, as well as a couple hundred thousand refugees from the New Orleans area who were staying with extended family or in overcrowded hotel rooms. The result was that Baton Rouge was tremendously overcrowded and overwhelmed by its sudden influx in population. Traffic was a disaster of its own, and driving anywhere in the city could take hours. This unfortunate fact made attending meetings, getting supplies, or moving personnel extremely hard. Landing an aircraft at Baton Rouge airport was a challenge, and once permission to land was received, there was often nowhere to park the aircraft.

From Baton Rouge, conducting the Coast Guard rescue and response operation and returning the Mississippi River to commerce would have been exceedingly difficult. The quick response and tremendous flexibility which made the Sector operation a success would not have been possible with the limitations of post-Katrina Baton Rouge. In Alexandria we quickly expanded to take up the entire convention center as the temporary Sector command center. We also had full use of the retired England Air Force Base. At one point we had more than thirty Coast Guard and auxiliary aircraft flying in and out of the former base and using all the ramp space they needed. We had full computer and phone access, we had good accommodations, and critical marine industry leaders could easily operate alongside the Coast Guard in Alexandria as well, often working inside the command center. In hindsight, Alexandria was perfect.

Although important governmental events and decisions were happening in Baton Rouge, the Coast Guard was still able to take part, as a result of our liaison officer system. Lieutenant Valerie Boyd was assigned to the Governor's Office of Homeland Security and Emergency Preparedness (GOHSEP). She arrived in Baton Rouge the day before Katrina hit New Orleans and set up her watch team of Coasties in the new center. Lieutenant Boyd served as the primary source of information between the Coast Guard and the many agencies that made up the GOHSEP. With the Coast Guard playing a lead role in the rescue operation, she worked closely with the Louisiana National Guard, the Louisiana Department of Wildlife and Fisheries, the Louisiana State Police, FEMA, the National Disaster Medical System, the Disaster Mortuary Operational Response Team, the Civil Air Patrol, and others and ensured Coast Guard operations were well coordinated with each agency. She also ran the Coast Guard detachment working in the GOHSEP. She excelled at managing this team of over forty Coasties trained in search and rescue, air operations, surface operations, marine safety, and communications.

Lieutenant Boyd's impact on the overall operation was essential. Her coordination of the Coast Guard and National Guard operations is a clear example of the importance of her role. While the Coasties in the boats rescued stranded people from their rooftops and brought them to dry land, she arranged for the National Guard to meet the Coast Guard boats and transport the survivors to safety. Another example would be the No Fly Zone she initiated over New Orleans through the Federal Aviation Administration offices in Houston. This No Fly Zone was to keep all civilian aircraft within ten miles of New Orleans flying above three thousand feet and ensured the safety of the dozens of helicopters hoisting survivors all over the city. She also requested a large military airplane to serve as a communications platform over the city for the helicopters. This was critical in relaying medevac information to both Coast Guard and National Guard helicopters as the rescue operation began. She worked to develop staging areas for medical treatment and even triaged 9-1-1 calls and directed resources in response.

In New Orleans, Lieutenant Commander Cheri Ben-Iesau was assigned as the Coast Guard liaison with the City of New Orleans to convey information between the City and our Sector command center in Alexandria. She rode out the storm in City Hall and endured the ensuing deprivations, days with little food, no sanitary facilities, and the threat of attack by the roving bands of looters and criminals. As the destruction of the city became apparent, city officials needed serious help and Ben-Iesau stepped up, far beyond her expected duties as the Coast Guard liaison. She ended up serving as the principal liaison for a number of local, state, and federal response agencies, including the National Guard, the Louisiana State Police, local parish sheriffs, the FBI, and various fire departments simply because she was on scene and had the authority to speak for the Coast Guard and make things happen. Like Lieutenant Boyd, she even fielded and triaged 9-1-1 calls, directing personnel and resources to respond. Without question, the two liaison officers were directly responsible for saving countless lives as they directed rescue teams in response to 9-1-1 calls. But on a larger scale, Ben-Iesau saved thousands more as she provided critical input to help direct the initial overall Coast Guard strategy.

Neither Lieutenant Boyd nor Lieutenant Commander Ben-Iesau were trained for any of these critical tasks, nor did they have any experience to guide them. But Coasties are trained to act independently as needed and make decisions on their own. These two exceptional officers, with this culture of independent action steeped in their Coast Guard hearts, were essential to the response of the Sector command center. For the captains and decision makers in Alexandria, having their direct insight into the concerns, discussions, and solutions in both Baton Rouge and City Hall was invaluable. Both liaison officers were also kept fully informed of Sector operations and had the authority to commit Coast Guard forces, boats, ships,

The Industrial Canal shortly after the levee broke, utterly destroying the Lower 9th Ward of New Orleans. Watching this water slam into this huge neighborhood brought home to me the extent of the tragedy and the unimaginable rescue operation we must mount to save these people, many of whom we could already see gathering on rooftops. The power of the water was staggering. Houses near the breech were lifted off their foundations and carried several blocks away by the force of the water. (USCG, Captain Robert Mueller)

helicopters, and security teams as needed and without question from the commanders and captains back at the command center. If the liaison officers said it was needed immediately, the command center made it happen even quicker. This is typically not done in military circles, where important decisions are often made at higher levels, but this delegated authority greatly facilitated the amazing flexibility of the entire Coast Guard response. This worked the other way as well. The liaison officers could quickly arrange coordination with other agency resources and personnel to meet Coast Guard operational needs.

And the smooth way all of this worked was yet another affirmation of the Continuity of Operations Plan developed by Commander Greg Depinet and Lieutenant Commander

Jimmy Duckworth. They couldn't possibly have foreseen what was going to happen during Katrina, but they built a flexible framework that put the right people in the right places and could be expanded and adapted as needed.

On the operations side, things were ramping up quickly. Despite serious communications problems, the command center had accounted for most of the small boat crews scattered across Louisiana and Mississippi. A number of cell phone towers were down or disabled and land lines were becoming a real issue as well with the increasing flooding, but eventually all units checked in and reported their status.

It was nerve-racking waiting for the units to report, probably made more so by the newly combined nature of the Sector. Because not everyone knew each other yet, a comfortable working knowledge and rhythm had yet to develop. The safety of the families was also a huge issue. Many were at Alexandria with the main Sector staff, but some had gone to the Naval Air Station in Jackson, Mississippi, which had lost power due to tornadoes knocking down trees in the area. This made it difficult to get an accurate count of whose family was now safe and who might still be in transit somewhere on the road. With the damage reports starting to come in, there were a lot of Coasties on duty who were very worried about the safety of their families. Eventually, all reported in safe, but in some cases it was a couple of very long and worrisome days before the Coastie on duty, working to save others, found out if his or her own family was okay.

Even as we waited for news of our families, we were very pleased that all boats and crews survived with minimal damage, though most could have used a chainsaw as part of their equipment to cut their way through the fallen trees to get to the water and launch their boats. This was one of many lessons learned for future storms; all small boat crews would henceforth be equipped with chainsaws, fuel, and an extra chainsaw bar and chain. For the moment, many of the boat crews struggled to get their boats to a launch. Some were able to borrow a chainsaw, but many had to move trees by hand or maneuver their trucks and boats around the obstacles, a very messy business with the acres of mud left by the torrential rain that came with the storm. It was estimated later that fifty percent of the trees in the heavily treed St. Tammany Parish came down in Katrina. Other parishes and counties had similar numbers. Just as an example, my house in Mandeville lost 12 of 18 trees in the storm. The few survivors in my yard were scrawny little things; all the big trees came down, including two pine trees more than fifty years old. Some of the pine trees snapped about one-third or halfway up, as pine trees often do in hurricanes. But many were simply uprooted, which normally would have been unusual, but heavy rains inundated the area for a couple of weeks before Katrina hit, saturating the ground with water and making the trees more vulnerable to falling over in the mud. An uprooted tree is much harder to move than one that has simply snapped off, as the root systems encased in dirt are very heavy and often half-buried.

Further complicating the transit of the boat crews to the water were the tornadoes that accompanied Katrina. From the air you could clearly see the paths of the twisters. After the storm, nearly all the trees were down in a straight line from the sheer and constant force of the hurricane winds. On the north shore of the lake that meant the trees usually fell to the south, all in neat rows. But where a tornado went through, they fell in all different directions, and while interesting from the air, it made life very difficult for the boat crews on the ground trying to get around this mess.

Despite their own challenges, many of the boat crews immediately undertook rescues, helping people in serious need as they worked their way to the water. "The Lifesavers" are how Coasties think of themselves. There are many different missions for this smallest of the armed forces, including homeland security, oil pollution response, aids to navigation, marine inspection, ice breaking, drug interdiction, fisheries protection, marine safety, and environmental protection, and most Coasties operate across many of these missions. But from boot camp to the very highest levels in the service, life-saving has always been the core, the heart, of the Coast Guard. As a military service, Coasties have served in every war since 1790, often in very dangerous missions. In the Iraq War, the Coast Guard patrol boats patrolled *in front* of the Navy minesweepers to protect them from shore fire while the minesweepers cleared mines to protect the large merchant ships behind them with supplies for the Army and Air Force. With Saddam Hussein having thousands of mines deployed or ready to deploy to stop the U.S. ships, the minesweepers were essential to getting the huge supply ships loaded with tanks, ammunition, and fuel safely into port. However, patrolling in front of the minesweepers was very dangerous indeed, and the Coasties on those boats realized they were expendable. They also played a large role in stopping those mines from being deployed, seizing barges full of mines and finding more in caves with their operators. But even with missions of that importance, life-saving trumps everything. There is an unwritten code in the Coast Guard, "You have to go out, but you don't have to come back," meaning that if someone is in trouble, you have to go out to rescue them, even if you might not make it back alive. That ethos of doing everything possible to save the lives of complete strangers is written on every Coast Guard heart. And during Katrina, those hearts were working overtime.

I, too, wanted to get into the city immediately and take part in the rescue, but my place was in Alexandria to get resources and people flowing into the city. The command center, otherwise known as the "Watch," did an amazing job. With everybody working twelve-hour shifts around the clock, and often fifteen- to eighteen-hour shifts, particularly at shift change, it didn't take long for things to start moving. Of the three main components of the Incident Command Structure we were using, logistics was primary. Everything from food and water to bullets and hand wipes to fuel and plastic bags had to be taken into the city. We didn't foresee it, and it's hard to believe even now, but absolutely nothing was available in or around the city to support our operations. Every single thing any Coastie would need with him or her in the city had to be carried there: every snack, every drop of drinking water, every gallon of fuel, all tools, oil for engines, socks, changes of clothes, every ounce of washing water, underwear, sunscreen, hand wipes, paper towels, toothpaste, pencils, paper, maps. In short, every single thing had to be thought of ahead of time, purchased or otherwise acquired, and then carried down into the city. The Watch did an amazing job of both moving forces into the destruction zone and figuring out what they would need once they were there. Everyone moved at a frantic pace, overwhelmed by the sense that people were dying out there and we had to save them. Even a slight delay could make the difference between life and death for people just barely hanging on, desperate souls praying for somebody to come rescue them.

It quickly became apparent that at the pace we had set, finding meals to eat was something we didn't have time for, so the Coast Guard spouses stepped up and worked with local businesses to deliver food to the Watch. We were not authorized to spend Coast Guard funds on food. Regulations required each Coast Guard member to buy food individually and submit a travel claim for expenses at some later date. Obviously this typical government paperwork drill was impossible given the circumstances, and many of the younger Coasties didn't have the money to front the government for a month or two of meals as well as all the incidental expenses that crop up when you are away from home. Junior enlisted members of all military branches are paid very little, and if they have a family, some rely on food stamps just to survive. Happily, the spouses worked with the business leaders of Alexandria, who were very generous and eager to assist.

Sleep became an issue too. Frank and I often had to order

Admiral Duncan is briefed while visiting the Alexandria command center. We covered the walls with maps and charts to help us display and process the huge volumes of information flowing into and out of the many operations required in our Katrina effort. (USCG)

people to leave the Watch floor after being relieved and to go to bed. From what we had seen in the city on that first helicopter ride, we knew this was going to be a marathon, and all of our people were sprinting just as hard as they could to get the rescue operation moving. It was difficult for some, but when a captain gives an order, it is to be obeyed. If only we could have ordered them to actually sleep instead of lying in bed awake with their minds racing.

Fortunately we had overwhelming support from our parent command, the Coast Guard Eighth District, and indeed the entire Coast Guard was focused on supporting Sector New Orleans in this effort. The Eighth District, then led by Rear Admiral Robert Duncan, was responsible for all Coast Guard operations in the states along the Gulf Coast as well as the twenty-three or so states that border or feed into the Mississippi River system. Admiral Duncan and his staff were headquartered in downtown New Orleans, but for Katrina they had relocated to St. Louis, and from there they did exceptional work in supporting and supplying not only our efforts, but rescue and recovery operations across the entire Gulf Coast. Admiral Duncan himself was traveling quite a bit, as he was needed at the highest levels at federal, state, and regional meetings and planning efforts. Captain Joe Castillo (soon promoted to Rear Admiral), his operations officer, traveled with the admiral and served as his point man for the actual operations in New Orleans. In this role, Captain Castillo was invaluable. He had previously been the Commanding Officer at Group New Orleans, and he was intimately familiar with the New Orleans area and what would be needed for the rapidly building rescue operation.

Captain Kevin Marshall was Eighth District Chief of Staff, running things in St. Louis and throughout the entire district. The D8 staff, while refugees themselves in St. Louis, provided tremendous support and soon had planeloads and truckloads of supplies headed to support the efforts in New Orleans. The staff also worked closely with the next level up, the Coast Guard Atlantic Area Command in Portsmouth, Virginia, who led the Coast Guard effort east of the Rocky Mountains. While normally moving large amounts of equipment, supplies, and personnel would take a blizzard of paperwork and long delays for processing, the D8 staff smoothed the road with the Atlantic Area staff and ultimately with Coast Guard Headquarters in Washington. I can't tell you exactly what they did or who did it, but from my own time serving at various staff levels, I know that these dedicated men and women moved bureaucratic mountains and got the critical equipment, supplies, and personnel flowing to us right from the start. For example, they managed to secure our access to the Coast Guard Aviation Training Center in Mobile, Alabama. Although Sector Mobile itself had been impacted by the storm, the Eighth District immediately worked with headquarters in Washington to make the helicopters and aircraft at the Aviation Training

Center available for the New Orleans operation. This was essential, not only for the support provided by the aircraft and their highly experienced aircrews who normally served as instructors, but for the use of the large maintenance facilities, where most Coast Guard aircraft would receive maintenance and repair during the rescue operation.

In some ways, I think the small size of the Coast Guard really helped us respond so quickly. With only about six thousand officers, there are many close and longstanding relationships in the senior officer corps. For example, Captain Frank Paskewich I were in the same company at the Coast Guard Academy from 1979 to 1981. Captain Terry Gilbreath, the Commanding Officer of MSU Morgan City, who stood the night watch at the Sector headquarters in Alexandria, was class of 1983. We had known each other at the Academy and

A severely damaged oil platform in the Gulf of Mexico. Despite serious damage to many oil platforms and drilling rigs out in the Gulf, there were no significant oil spills offshore. (USCG)

later worked very closely together in Mobile. Captain Pete Simons, from the D8 staff, a lawyer by trade and jack-of-all-trades on the Alexandria staff, was a classmate of mine. Air Station Mobile, where the helicopters were serviced, was commanded by another classmate, Captain Dave Callahan. Captain Joe Castillo, who was traveling with Admiral Robert Duncan, was another close friend. We served in Puerto Rico together and trusted each other completely. And so it went. We all had friends on the D8 staff, Area staff, and at headquarters. They knew us and we knew them, and things work much smoother when you know who you are working with.

With such connections, D8 began immediately funneling people, boats, and supplies to New Orleans. The DART teams with their small aluminum flood punts from Coast Guard units along the Mississippi and Ohio Rivers were among the first to arrive. Right on their heels were small boat crews, logistics experts, yeomen for paperwork, surface operations experts, aviators to help on the Watch, communications experts, security personnel for the boats, mechanics, and more. It seemed like the entire Coast Guard was helping in any way it could, and D8 was arranging for and sending down the support we desperately needed to run what was quickly becoming a massive rescue operation. Without a doubt the D8 staff were unseen and unsung heroes in the widely successful Coast Guard operation, not only in and around New Orleans, but along the entire Gulf Coast.

In addition to the rescue operation, a huge oil pollution clean-up operation was unfolding along the inland waterways and in the bayous. These spills were from the refineries and other installations damaged by the huge storm surge. At the Murphy Oil Refinery in Chalmette, the massive oil tanks had been ruptured by the wave coming up the river, spreading oil throughout the parish. Oil is less dense than water, and it floated on top of the thirteen feet of water already in Chalmette, making dramatically worse what already seemed like total devastation. Those houses both flooded and oiled

Massive oil tanks shoved off their mountings and cracked by the storm surge. The oil spills were tremendous in various locations throughout the bayou. The safest and most environmentally friendly way to clean up the oil is by burning it, as the process produces fertilizer and the marsh grows back fairly quickly. The marsh in the background had been set on fire as part of the clean-up effort. (USCG)

were ruined forever. Chalmette was a very tight-knit family community, and some families saw not only their own home ruined but those of their extended families: the homes of their mothers, brothers and sisters, aunts and uncles. Entire families lost everything they owned, and it would take months and years for restitution to come. Some Sector personnel lived in Chalmette. They and their families lost everything as well. Yet they kept working at a frantic pace. Our command secretary, Mrs. Edie Landry, was one who lost everything, but she kept focused on the mission. She will always be a hero to me.

By Day Three, the Watch was getting calls from the White House to reopen the Mississippi River. The river itself was a mess, with all the buoys and landside aids to navigation missing. These signposts are critical to navigating large

Two large pogy fishing boats deposited in the middle of the main highway from New Orleans to Venice by the storm surge. The boats were still tied together. To return them to the water, huge inflatable rollers were placed under them and slowly inflated. The boats were then slowly rolled back to the water. This was but a very small part of the greatest marine salvage operation since Pearl Harbor. (USCG)

ships in the Mississippi's tight and twisting channels. If there are no aids, then ships don't move. Getting these aids back into place was estimated to take about three months. But this was unacceptable. The grain harvest for the nation was piling up on the docks in St. Louis, and there was no place left to put it. All the grain storage elevators were full and the barges were too. They needed to start shipping the grain down the river and out to the world. Even in the midst of an unprecedented disaster, America's superhighway could not remain closed for long.

Frank was dealing with the largest ever oil spill situation in the lower forty-eight states, the largest waterways shutdown and restoration disaster ever, the largest offshore crisis ever, and I was working the largest rescue operation ever. As Frank said, "Everything is Biblical proportions!"

Meanwhile, Back at the Ranch

Things at Station New Orleans were hopping, to say the least. The initial seven Coasties who had made the trip across the lake were soon joined by station personnel from Coast Guard Sector Houston/Galveston, the first of hundreds and then thousands of Coasties from around the nation who would join the rescue effort. More station personnel arrived by truck across the Causeway Bridge, along with Station Venice and Station Grand Isle personnel, and Coast Guard Station New Orleans came back to life.

At the makeshift Sector New Orleans headquarters in the hotel and convention center in Alexandria, Louisiana, the captains knew that Station New Orleans would become a major hub for the rapidly expanding surface rescue operations. The station building itself was largely intact, except for the critical boat repair tools and parts that were flooded on the ground floor and the now closed-off areas destroyed by the vandals. However, the command center, boat docks, large parking areas, radios, fuel tanks, water systems, and other basic infrastructure were key to the staging of the rescue mission.

Other Coast Guard units in New Orleans did not weather the storm as well or were not capable of rescue operations. The Coast Guard Integrated Support Command, a major repair and support facility at the Industrial Canal, was underwater, along with its badly needed tools, shops, and spare parts. The Regional Exam Center, where U.S. mariner's licenses are kept and exams given, was also underwater. The other major division of Sector, the former Marine Safety Office, was located in the upper floors of a building across from the Superdome. Comprised of only office spaces, it did have one benefit. Weapons, badly needed to protect the crews undertaking rescue operations, were stored there. When the administrators of the building couldn't be reached, not surprising in those frantic days, the Coasties were forced to break into the building and walk up many flights of stairs to their dark offices and the safe with the valuable rifles, shotguns, and pistols. These weapons were absolutely critical in protecting the crews in the little DART rescue boats and made small boat operations possible. Coast Guard Air Station New Orleans, located on the Joint Reserve Base in Belle Chasse, south of the city on the west bank of the river, was not flooded and was vital to the helicopter rescue operations that were ramping up. But it was on the far side of town, not easily accessible by land from the station, and nowhere near the flooded parts of the city, so boat forces could not be staged from there.

Initially the focus was turning the forty-man small boat rescue station that was Station New Orleans into a major hub for rescue operations throughout the city. As the storm passed and the first images of the rapidly flooding city were seen nationally on Fox and CNN, small boat stations all around the nation prepared to send personnel and equipment to New Orleans. The vast majority of highly trained boat rescue personnel were assigned to the small boat stations in coastal areas around the country, but stations along the Gulf Coast, particularly those east of New Orleans, had their own problems to deal with. Sector Mobile in Alabama had flooding issues of its own, with some areas of Mobile Bay seeing ten feet of floodwater. They were also coping with major storm damage in areas near Station Dauphin Island (Alabama) and Station Pensacola (Florida) and even had issues in Station Destin, way over in the Florida panhandle. Closer to New Orleans, Station Pascagoula was damaged and dealing with catastrophic flooding on the Mississippi coast.

Station Gulfport, part of Sector New Orleans and just across the state line in Mississippi, was simply gone. Station Gulfport had been a fairly new, heavily reinforced concrete structure up on stilts, designed to easily withstand Category 4 hurricane winds and flooding. But nothing could withstand the thirty-foot wall of water that slammed into Gulfport that day. The station was completely washed away, wiped clean. Like the Sector New Orleans units, however, the boats and personnel were safely evacuated, and they were available for duty. They were soon working around the clock in rescue operations, but for the time being, and for several weeks to come, Station Gulfport existed only in the hearts and minds of those who had called it home.

Station Venice, down toward the mouth of the Mississippi River and normally working rescue and fisheries enforcement, was built very much like Station Gulfport. It was designed to

Station Gulfport was completely destroyed, but its crew rescued hundreds in New Orleans and in Mississippi. (USCG)

withstand the same Category 4 winds and flooding. The building at Station Venice was still standing after Katrina passed, but it was a total wreck. Everything under the building, which included boat parts and tools, was lost in the intense and very fast-moving flooding Mississippi River, which ravaged the entire Venice area. Piles of trashed vegetation were everywhere, along with all kinds of debris. The building itself stood, but the roof had caved in, and everything inside the building was soaked. With the intense heat of a typical Louisiana summer, anything even slightly damp was soon covered in mold. Floors, counters, kitchen equipment, beds, radios, desks, carpets, drywall, ceilings—it was all covered in mold and ruined.

Station Grand Isle, on the Louisiana Gulf Coast south of New Orleans, was also severely flooded. Its buildings were standing but everything inside was destroyed, as were the houses on the base. Most of the island had been evacuated, but some of the Station Grand Isle crew undertook rescues on the island itself after the storm. With the only bridge connecting the island severely damaged, the Station Grand Isle crew also moved critical supplies to the island with their boats. The rest of the Station Grand Isle crew, along with the crew from Station Venice and some of the Station Gulfport crew, were temporarily assigned to Station New Orleans.

The Sector staff in Alexandria were funneling most incoming station rescue personnel to Station New Orleans, soon to be called Forward Operating Base New Orleans because it was growing exponentially. Coasties from all over the nation were arriving daily. In those days each Coast Guard unit had its name proudly emblazoned on the ball caps that members of that command wore. For example, the Station New Orleans crew wore Coast Guard-regulation blue ball caps that said "Station New Orleans" on the front in gold letters, while the Station Key West crew wore the same blue ball cap, but theirs said "Station Key West." As new personnel arrived, it was interesting to see at a glance where they were from. We had Coasties from stations and bases all over the United States, and it was heartwarming and encouraging to see what seemed like the entire Coast Guard turning out for this operation. We knew the locals on the Gulf Coast, those stations in Mississippi, Alabama, and the Florida panhandle had enough Katrina-related issues of their own to keep them very busy, but we had a large number of Coasties arriving from Texas and the East Coast, as well as DART boats from units upriver from us on the Mississippi River. District 9 came from the Great Lakes, and units arrived from New England and Puerto Rico and as far away as Alaska, California, and even Guam. Since Sector New Orleans had just been created, we didn't have a hat yet, but the crew from Station Grand Isle gave me one of their caps with the appropriate scrambled eggs on the brim for a captain to wear. Though it seems silly, with people from all over the Coast Guard arriving every day, wearing the correct rank insignia on the ball cap was important so that new people could see at a glance who was doing what. I wore that cap with pride throughout the rescue, partly as a reminder that even though their station was destroyed, we were all one Coast Guard working together.

The station Commanding Officer, Chief Warrant Officer Dan Brooks, managed this massive influx of people smoothly and efficiently. As the station berthing areas had been destroyed by the looters, incoming personnel pitched tents under the building. Some didn't have tents and slept in the open at first, establishing improvised campgrounds where many reconnected and reestablished professional relationships with old friends and shipmates. Food consisted of MREs, and like all prepackaged long-term storage food, it left something to be desired. Without question the MREs are several orders of magnitude better than the infamous C-rats military men and women ate in years past, and the variety was much appreciated, but MREs are only tasty for a limited time.

With the station building ravaged by looters, who urinated on beds and smeared feces on the walls, we set up tents and began camping under and around the station building. The tent city grew rapidly as hundreds of Coasties began arriving for the rescue operation. (USCG, Mike Howell)

Full rescue operations at Station New Orleans began almost immediately, with the station functioning as the headquarters for the entire surface rescue operation in the city. During the first three days after Katrina, there were several surface operations taking place simultaneously in New Orleans. River operations were being conducted by the larger Coast Guard small boats, the 41-footers and 55-footers that couldn't operate in the tight confines of the city. These boats were working with larger Coast Guard cutters on the river: construction tenders such as *Pamlico* and even major cutters like the *Harriet Lane* and *Spencer*, 270-foot cutters, and *Gallatin*, a 378-foot cutter of the largest and most sophisticated class of cutter in the Coast Guard at the time.

Ice rescue boats, basically high-powered air boats, from the Coast Guard Ninth District on the Great Lakes, had also deployed into the city. Gunner's Mate Master Chief Patrick O'Kelly brought down the team. They were a self-sustaining operation with RVs and their own supplies and did great rescue work those first days, saving hundreds. Later, when the water became too polluted, the ice boats had to be withdrawn. Their huge propellers were spraying the toxic waters in a fine mist, creating a health hazard. This was true for all airboats. After the water became toxic, they could no longer be used. The third operation was the Unified Command of Coast Guard and FEMA, based at Zephyr Field. The Coast Guard DART boats, specialized for flooded urban operations, worked there from the very beginning. There were so many things to coordinate: boat crews to be formed and then matched to boats, MSST and later PSU security teams to be assigned to boats or groups of boats, supplies matched to crews, maintenance for boats and engines to be assigned, and a myriad of other details required to keep a large operation running smoothly.

The crews based at the station began with the Bucktown neighborhood right next to the station and quickly moved into the seriously flooded Lakeview neighborhood, where many were stranded in their attics or on their roofs. Station operations would eventually include parts of the north shore of the lake in the Eden Isles area of Slidell, the Venetian Isles area near Chef Pass, the Rigolets, and the far eastern communities of Hopedale and Shell Beach in St. Bernard Parish. While the station didn't have the very shallow-draft flood punts of the DART teams, they conducted thousands of rescues in the deeper waters of the lake and Gulf areas.

Station New Orleans crews also rescued about 2,200 desperate people stranded on the high ground near the levee at the University of New Orleans. Boatswain's Mate Second Class Jessica Guidroz took command of a twelve-boat flotilla composed of ten Coast Guard boats and two auxiliary boats from the volunteer arm of the Coast Guard and was soon rescuing people from the university and transporting them to Station New Orleans for further transport out of the city. Though she was a bit junior for such a large task, she had exceptional local knowledge and a strong command presence that made her a perfect fit for the job. It took six long days to complete the evacuations at the university, and like every other boat operation in the city, the crews were exceeding and often doubling the official Coast Guard safety standards for how long a crew could operate without rest. They were also far exceeding how many people they could transport in their boats, but with so many people needing rescue and the benefit of calm waters, they did what they needed to do.

On day four of this six-day operation, the remaining people on the beach by the university began to riot. They turned on

This 25-foot rescue boat was used on Lake Pontchartrain to rescue more than two thousand people trapped on the levee next to the University of New Orleans. (USCG, Mike Howell)

the eighteen New Orleans firefighters who were trying to maintain order and help the people safely into the boats. The firefighters had to evacuate, along with a young woman and her small child who seemed to be the focus of intense anger by the now violent mob, all rescued by BM2 Jessica Guidroz. With the firefighters now on the boats, there was no assistance on shore for the Coasties. With her boat some distance from the shore, Guidroz got on the loud speaker and told the people that they would not be rescued unless they restored order themselves. The riot continued with people shouting obscenities and throwing things, and Guidroz turned the entire flotilla around and started to depart the area. The crowd immediately calmed down and began to form themselves into lines for rescue. Seeing this, Guidroz returned and resumed rescue operations, saving every single person and transporting them to safety.

Sector personnel at the makeshift headquarters in Alexandria were matching the pace set by the station crews and were working around the clock to send supplies to the Coasties in New Orleans as quickly as they could. However, many essentials were hard to come by in the immediate aftermath of the storm. Obviously there were no supplies to be had in and around New Orleans; the devastation there was complete. Since the hurricane passed east of New Orleans, there weren't any supplies available in that direction either. But even north and west of the city, civilian companies were closed, warehouses were boarded up, and stores were shuttered, their personnel evacuated. Not much was available in those first few days. Yet sometimes minor miracles happened just when they were needed the most.

Fuel had become a major issue by the third day of the rescue operation. The Sector staff was working the problem in Alexandria, but finding companies willing to bring trucks full of highly flammable gasoline into New Orleans was difficult. The boat crews had quickly used up the fuel in their boats getting to the station and conducting rescues in the immediate area. They had then used up the fuel in the station's fuel tank running continuous boat operations. That fuel tank would normally last six weeks of operations, but it had been emptied in two days. As a last resort, they were siphoning fuel out of their own personal cars, which had been destroyed by the storm. Though their cars had flooded and were now useless hulks, the fuel tanks still held some precious gasoline and the boat crews were siphoning out this fuel to keep the boats running. But now even those tanks were empty. Rescue operations would be coming to a halt very soon unless something happened, and quickly.

Then a tanker truck showed up, out of nowhere, driving down the levee. The driver hopped out and asked if we could use some gasoline! He had a full truck and had felt led to come to New Orleans to help out. He had driven alone through the empty cities of Covington and Mandeville on the north shore of the lake, then across the deserted Causeway Bridge to New Orleans. When he reached the end of the long bridge, he found the streets below flooded and impassable. So he decided to turn left on the levee and drive along the top of the levee for a while, finally reaching the station and providing badly needed fuel to keep the rescue boats running. I asked him if he wasn't scared to bring a truck of explosive gasoline into a city rocked by looting and riots. He smiled and said, "Naw, I've got a shotgun in the seat next to me and the Lord was with me."

This was a pivotal moment for me. As we rapidly ramped up the rescue operation and I realized the magnitude of the disaster response I was leading, that very first day in the helicopter I had prayed, "Lord, I can't do this myself. I need some help here; you gotta make this work." Not the most formal of prayers, but it was very heartfelt, and I think that is what matters most. This fuel truck, coming out of nowhere at just the right time, not contracted for by anyone, was my first real indication that the Lord was with us. It would definitely not be the last.

After the hurricane passed, many vessels in the harbor were damaged or sunk. The upper level of the world-famous Southern Yacht Club was on fire, while the lower floor was underwater. (USCG, Mike Howell)

A boat full of survivors rescued by Coasties after Katrina. (USCG)

A Coast Guard MSST member, fully armed and ready to go. These heavily armed Coasties provided security in the little boats and were ordered to look "mean and ugly" to intimidate would-be trouble makers. The deterrent was very effective. No boats operating with an MSST were targeted by gunfire. (USCG, PA1 Bauman)

This photo depicts the height of the water at the peak of the massive storm surge that came rushing into New Orleans. After the storm passed, the water would slowly drain out of New Orleans, back into Lake Pontchartrain and the Gulf of Mexico, and the water level would stabilize at the height of the lake's normal water level, leaving the well-known "bathtub ring" that could be seen throughout the city for years after the storm. (USCG)

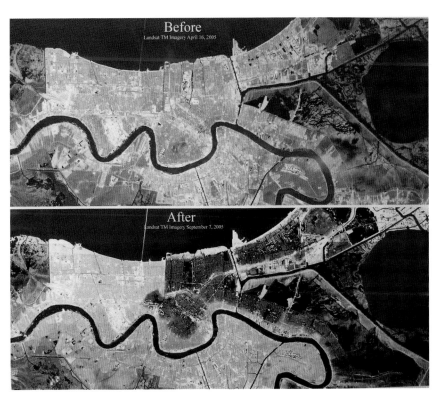

Pre-Katrina and post-Katrina satellite images of New Orleans. The dark areas on the bottom map are the flooded zones. (USCG)

Coast Guard and volunteer FEMA crews worked together on the small flood punts to save lives. (USCG)

Like most rescue crews on the small flood punts, this boat was comprised of a mixed crew of FEMA volunteers, Coast Guard regulars, and an armed Coast Guard Port Security Unit (PSU) member, in camouflage, providing the security presence. (USCG)

A large ship shoved up onto the batture, that narrow strip of land between the levee and the river, forced there by the storm surge rushing up the river. Several tug boats pulled it back into the river before the water level receded too much; otherwise it would have become a permanent monument. (USCG, Captain Robert Mueller)

These two towboats were manned during the storm, and the crews had a terrifying ride as the surge ripped them away from their moorings and flung them across the river and onto the levee. The plywood over the wheelhouse windows speaks volumes about the dangers from the waves. (Mike Marshall)

A fishing fleet destroyed by the storm surge. Some of these fishermen lived on their vessels and couldn't afford insurance. Like many in New Orleans, they suddenly found themselves with no home and no income, a very difficult combination. (USCG)

A typical FEMA/Coast Guard team. This photo shows FEMA firefighters working in an orange Coast Guard rescue boat. (USCG, PA1 Bauer)

The breech in the 17th Street Canal Levee. The Bucktown neighbor-hood, in the foreground, has three feet of water flooding it from the overtopping of the Lake Pontchartrain levee. The Lakeview neighbor-hood, behind the breech, was rapidly flooded with more than fifteen feet of water. (USCG, Captain Robert Mueller)

A rescue mission underway. (USCG, PA1 Bauer)

A man and his guitar. (USCG, PA1 Bauman)

A six-block-long debris pile in Lakeview that rose three stories high. This debris pile remained for months as people gutted their flooded homes. The smell from the rotting food in the refrigerators was stomach churning. (USCG photo, Rear Admiral Joseph Castillo)

A dwindling fuel supply was not the only challenge facing the rescue teams. Security for the little boats operating in the flooded streets of the city had become a real issue. The answer was in the Coast Guard Maritime Safety and Security Teams, MSSTs. These small boat units were highly trained and equipped for security missions. Designed to deploy with their heavily armed 25-foot boats, they helped to ensure the security of Super Bowl games, presidential election conventions, major diplomatic visits such as the G8 summits, and other high-profile national level events located near the water. These units were quickly deployed to New Orleans, but I requested most come without their boats. While superb for harbor, river, and near-shore coastal operations, the 25-foot boats were far too big and heavy for operations on the flooded streets of the city. However, the MSST personnel were perfect for the security mission in the little flood punts. These MSST Coasties were wearing full-body armor and were armed with fully automatic M4 rifles and M9 pistols. I told them plainly to look "mean and ugly" in the boats and to make sure they could be clearly seen as a deterrent. It worked superbly.

Lieutenant Commander Sean Regan, Commanding Officer of the New Orleans MSST, established both the operational and logistical procedures for these critical security operations. Soon Coast Guard MSSTs from all over the nation would arrive in New Orleans, and they were placed under Regan as the local expert. This wasn't initially popular with the commanding officers of the other MSSTs, but I explained to them that with the rapidly expanding security operations, we needed a single point of contact with local knowledge, and Regan was it. Once everyone accepted this, the security missions ran very smoothly, and Regan did an exceptional job, working far above his paygrade to take care of all the MSST issues, requirements, and concerns.

The MSSTs were campers like everybody else at Station New Orleans. With the remains of the destroyed lakefront restaurants scattered all over the station grounds, each of the MSSTs found a large piece of wood and spray-painted their unit on it to define who they were and where they were camping: "Welcome to MSST Galveston Country" or "MSST Honolulu." These young Coasties were proud of their units and their mission. It added a little life and some smiles to the tent city that had sprung up.

Like the security operations, a single point of contact for all station-related matters was needed, and the local station Commanding Officer, CWO Dan Brooks, was so designated. As might be imagined, that caused some wounded egos, especially as some of the incoming officers outranked Chief Warrant Officer Brooks and expected to be placed in charge. But I needed an expert in station operations, an expert in the local area, and someone intimately familiar with Station New Orleans itself. Perhaps most importantly, I needed an officer who would be there for the duration of the operation as the

MSST New Orleans (NOLA) shows unit pride. (USCG, Mike Howell)

temporary-duty Coasties came and went. Obviously that position could only be filled by Brooks. As expected, Brooks did an amazing job keeping this rapidly expanding operation focused and operating smoothly. The station went from being looted to hosting over five hundred personnel in just a week, and he handled the many and sundry issues with professionalism and grace. I was particularly pleased when I noticed he was careful to always address more senior officers as "Sir" while he was politely giving them direction.

Such rank inversions were common during the operation as permanently assigned personnel with knowledge of the area were placed in leading positions, often over higher ranking temporary personnel. Given the magnitude of the disaster and the way regional conditions, logistics, and even topography influenced everything, local knowledge was critical to our operations. For example, on the river, the Lower 9 Mile Anchorage is near Meraux, around mile marker 82 on the river, close to Lower Coast Algiers and near English Turn, and that area can be and is often referred to by any of these five names. With the temporary personnel often staying a week or so and then returning to their regular unit, having permanently assigned leaders made all operations run much smoother. Once the incoming temporary personnel understood these things, there were no issues. In a military organization where rank permeates everything, this was a real credit to every single Coastie who deployed to help with the rescue operations in New Orleans. The rescue mission was far more important than ego, and such humility and grace in the face of overwhelming disaster epitomized the very best in the Coast Guard.

With so many operations being run out of Station New Orleans, there were countless teams, boats, and supplies to coordinate. Then there were the logistical challenges of getting the crews where they needed to go, and delays were always unacceptable. When the sun came up the boats and rescue crews had to be underway. These efforts were led by

Commander Russell Davidson and Commander Adam Shaw. We playfully called them "Bacardi and Coke," because they were always working closely together and they always made good things happen, as noted by a popular TV commercial of the day. There were many others working this staff, like Petty Officer Gary Feathers, who were critical to keeping this operation going. Although none of them made a single rescue, many of the rescues made would not have been possible without their very hard work, sometimes almost around the clock.

In the midst of this, the One-Armed Bandit, Coast Guard Auxiliarist Mike Howell, was everywhere on the base at once. Due to the proven threat of gunfire, Coast Guard headquarters decided that the civilian Coast Guard auxiliary volunteers could not join any rescue missions. While Mike initially chaffed at this, he quickly made himself invaluable as Station New Orleans turned into Forward Operating Base New Orleans, Louisiana, or FOB NOLA for short. By Day Three, portable generators had arrived so Mike didn't have to power the station from his boat, though *Mañana* was still providing satellite TV, the only link to regular news footage of what was happening in New Orleans. This was a needed respite for the troops, who were getting worn out from the never-ending rescue operations. To be able to see the extent of the disaster and know they were part of the biggest rescue operation in our nation's history was very encouraging to them. The news channels were left running on the big TV in the galley 24 hours a day so that boat crews could catch a quick view of what was happening as they passed through to grab a snack. The galley itself wasn't operating as a full kitchen. The small station cook staff could never feed this crowd, but snacks and various drinks were available 24-7 for the crews.

Mike and his auxiliary buddies also provided essential local knowledge to hundreds of incoming Coasties, most of whom had never before been to New Orleans. Mike's cohorts helped to decode the city's arcane geographic designations, as many local names made little sense at all to newly arriving personnel, and yet they were absolute, well-defined, and long-accepted names for important locations. The auxiliarists also helped the rescue crews familiarize themselves with the layout of a city built along a winding river. Neighborhoods and communities were often separated by canals and various bridges, and with streets skirting these waterways, local knowledge was invaluable. Without such guidance crews could get lost, which was a minor annoyance, or they could get themselves into serious trouble.

Auxiliary members also provided their personal aircraft for Coast Guard use. I flew back and forth to the Sector command center in a number of such excellent airplanes. This allowed me to travel quickly between New Orleans and Alexandria without using a valuable helicopter that would be better used in rescues.

One thing Mike became famous for was his ever-present camera. Mike sensed that history was being made, and he could always be found with his personal camera propped on his fake arm, eye behind the camera, clicking away. Before he passed away several years later, Mike gave me several CDs of his pictures and asked me to put them in the book that he expected me to write someday. Many of his photos grace the pages of this book, bringing the stories to life in ways mere words cannot.

Mike and his camera were there on Day Three when President George W. Bush made a surprise visit to Station New Orleans. It's not fair that the press hammered the president for not visiting New Orleans sooner, because he did visit very early in the operation. I think perhaps they were irritated because he didn't bring any press with him on that first visit. But he was here. You can see Mike's photos of him with the crew. When Mike first pointed his camera toward the president, lens propped on his fake arm for balance, the Secret Service rushed Mike but relaxed after examining both the camera and his fake arm.

Unfortunately I missed the visit, having just left for Alexandria to work supply issues. Obviously the president's movements in such a dangerous environment had to be kept secret, and it was a very quickly arranged visit. The Secret Service called the station to make the arrangements since the Coast Guard station was the only safe place in the city at that point, and he arrived by helicopter. The Coasties were thrilled. Shaking the president's hand and hearing him thank them for their heroism really boosted the morale of those who were working so very hard to save others.

The intense desire of these young men and women to rescue every single person they could, no matter what, was inspiring. Many of the Station New Orleans crew had lost

President George W. Bush visiting Station New Orleans on Day Three. The president didn't bring the press with him on his surprise visit, when he showed deep concern for the welfare of the Coast Guard men and women and intense support for what they were doing. (USCG, Mike Howell)

everything they owned. Many lost their homes and apartments in the flood itself. Then they lost their cars when the water came rushing in beneath the station. Since the station had never flooded before, it had seemed like a safe place to leave their cars as they evacuated with the Coast Guard rescue boats before the approaching storm. But when the water came in and submerged their cars, each was a total loss. For some it was the first car they had ever owned. Some of the crew even lost the change of clothes and few items they stored in the duty rooms at the station, where they slept when they were standing 24-hour duty in normal times. But the looters took care of that, stealing what they could and destroying the rest.

Yet these brave young men and women were like rescue machines; they kept going and going and going. I remember having to order some to stop and get something to eat, to take a few minutes to rest before heading out again, when what they really wanted was to get back out there. And their commitment never wavered, even in the extreme conditions after Katrina. The heat was beyond oppressive. Every day seemed to be a beautiful cloudless day, highs in the upper 90s, with little wind and very high humidity from the standing water. The word "stifling" only begins to describe it. In such heat, the rescue teams had to work the boats around obstacles in the water, and when they came to rail tracks or other high land emerging from the floodwaters, they had to carry the boats across to the water on the other side. It was exhausting work, and yet they were driven to go and go and go, not stopping for anything. There are those who say the younger generation of Coasties isn't as good as the old-timers. This is utterly ridiculous. The Coasties who worked in the Katrina rescue were titans, young people of tremendous strength. They proved to be highly resourceful, smart, and utterly dedicated. Without a doubt they are leaders of the highest quality. The future of the Coast Guard is very secure indeed!

The heat wasn't the only environmental factor with which the Coasties had to contend. With the waters becoming more polluted every day, cleanliness and sanitation were constant worries. When the waters flooded New Orleans, conditions deteriorated quickly. Everything that was in a garage—fertilizer, gasoline, oil, bug killer, paint, mineral spirits, glue—was immediately in the water. Sewage systems were compromised in various places, and raw sewage floated in the water too. Food from kitchens and household chemicals were also part of the mix. Add a few days of temperatures in the 90s, and it became a foul-smelling toxic stew. The smell from the water was nauseating, though you got used to it after a while. Thankfully, we became nose blind because the Coasties were in that sludge, wading in it at times, reaching into it, and getting splashed by it as they made rescues, day after day. The area was ripe for an outbreak of cholera, dysentery, or even Hepatitis C. Along with worrying about diseases, I also had major concerns about serious infections from even the slightest cut or skin laceration and feared foot rot, or jungle rot as it is sometimes known. Following the example of the British army in the Falklands War, I instructed officers to check the feet of those working under their charge to make sure foot rot didn't set in.

At one point the Centers for Disease Control from Atlanta came down to see how we were doing. They poked around the base and asked a lot of questions. One lady sampled and analyzed the air with a small machine she carried in a backpack. With dead animals and sometimes humans in the water, noxious chemicals and sewage contributing their own toxins, and air that stank so bad that new personnel were shocked, I was very worried about disease. It was a constant concern, and I half-jokingly asked the woman from the CDC if we were going to be okay. She smiled just a little and said, "We don't know. We're going to see what happens to you." I was taken aback for a moment when I realized she was quite serious. I had hoped for a better answer from the national experts on disease control.

Under such conditions, cleanliness was not just a necessity but a blessing. The first day or two *Mañana* provided showers, but her tanks ran dry and everybody resorted to using a one-liter bottle of water to clean themselves. Since water was in very short supply, only one bottle per person was allowed. Eventually we got access to greater supplies of water and would hose down people as they arrived at the gate from a long day of rescues. When a shower trailer showed up, contracted by the Sector up in Alexandria, it was a very welcome addition. Later still a laundry trailer arrived and it seemed like pure luxury; by that time we were all pretty strong smelling. Sector worked around the clock to keep the rescue forces supplied. They did an amazing job, but at times necessary provisions and the means to deliver them to the station simply weren't available. At least twice we nearly ran out of water but were saved by minor miracles in the form of unexpected and unaccounted for deliveries of water that had not been sent by Sector. I checked; nobody from Sector or anybody else could account for these badly needed supplies that arrived at just the right time.

Of course, it was not only humans who were suffering in the aftermath of the hurricane and its floods. We had rescued many dogs and cats from the ravaged city that were hopeful to meet their owners again. One little dog was famously reunited with its owner in Texas; I heard they made the cover of a major magazine. Others were less fortunate. One dog we brought to the base started to drink from the lake, which at that time was thoroughly mixed with polluted floodwater, and he started to get sick, then convulsed. After that we kept the animals away from any standing water. One news report claimed we were shooting dogs and cats instead of rescuing them. Nothing could be further from the truth. The rule was that if there was room in the boat and the animal looked half-civilized, we took the animal too. You have to remember that a lot of people stayed in New Orleans to ride out the storm because they wouldn't leave their pets behind. Now, having lost everything they owned, there was no way they were abandoning their beloved dog or cat to face the aftermath alone. Sometimes, when there were no people to be found, rescue teams returned with boatloads of animals. Fortunately the vast majority were scared and nervous but otherwise unharmed. In one case in Chalmette, a boat crew brought back three puppies that had been abandoned in a house.

Coasties absolutely love animals—many cutters and stations have mascots—and our base soon looked like a zoo. One huge bull mastiff puppy became quite the favorite and was quickly claimed by the newly arrived Port Security Unit (PSU). They gave the dog a camo hat with proper rank, and I understand he got both promoted and busted, depending on his performance. He stood guard duty with the PSU at the gate on top of the levee. This huge dog on duty with two

This bull mastiff puppy was rescued early during the operation and became the mascot of Port Security Unit 307. We rescued hundreds of dogs and cats, and several organizations helped reunite these pets with their owners. This particular dog was adopted by the PSU and immediately pressed into duty as a gate guard with his new family. (USCG, Mike Howell)

Coasties in camouflage and a mounted machine gun proved intimidating. Nearby gunfire at night stopped.

Before the PSU arrived, base security was iffy. We could sit and look out over the city and see complete darkness, total black, punctuated only by the flash of gunfire. We had no real fence, but there was one road in and out of the station that ran over the levee, and we put a checkpoint on it with what people we could spare. Our defenses were weak.

The Coast Guard Port Security Units have about 120 people each, most all of them reservists, meaning they work one weekend a month and two weeks of full-time training each year. But this is misleading. Many of the PSUs had been deployed in Iraq to protect the ports over there while American merchant and military ships unloaded critical war supplies. The PSUs also did other more "exciting" work, such as rooting heavily armed Iraqi Republican Guard zealots out of the caves near the waterways right as the war started, capturing the first prisoners of the war, and they came back fully qualified warriors.

These guys are the heavy hitters in all aspects of port security. They arrived in full camo, with tents, a kitchen, and supplies for a month. They came with everything they needed because they were trained and equipped to be fully deployable in a war zone, which seemed pretty appropriate at the moment. When they arrived, they solved several problems at once. They took over base security and improved it dramatically, and like the MSSTs, they provided security for the little flood punts, often riding in the FEMA boats with the firemen. Many of the pictures taken during the Katrina rescue of flood punts carrying camouflaged servicemen are Coasties from the PSU. I didn't worry about security anymore when the PSU showed up. Of interest, the PSU guys said New Orleans was worse than Iraq, because in Iraq, during the timeframe when they were there, it was easy to tell the good guys from the bad guys. In New Orleans, it wasn't obvious who was a good guy and who might shoot at the boat.

A member of PSU 307 in full gear. The PSU is the heavy hitter in Coast Guard security, designed to provide immediate emergency security for port facilities in a war zone. They come with tents, thirty days of supplies, and everything else they need for operations. PSU 307 deployed to New Orleans fresh from the war in Iraq, and these combat veterans were very much appreciated. (USCG, Mike Howell)

Captain Jeff Bauer of PSU 307 and Lieutenant Commander Sean Regan of MSST New Orleans were the men who made security happen, both at the base and on the water throughout the New Orleans rescue operation. (USCG, Mike Howell)

After several days of the servicemen and -women in the tent city surviving off MREs, another minor miracle occurred. The Professional Golfers' Association, or PGA, arrived and asked if we would allow them to set up a kitchen and prepare hot meals for the rescue workers. It was a complete surprise, and of course my answer was an immediate yes. They asked for an area to be cleared in the parking lot, and we moved campers to accommodate them. To our surprise, they set up a very nice tent and put a large kitchen in it. Then some of the golf pros and their wives showed up along with professional cooks and began cooking breakfast, lunch, and dinner. The food was excellent, and it was great for morale. After a hard day in the polluted and flooded city performing rescue ops, the boat crews could come in, get cleaned up, and get

The PGA set up a mess tent for us, providing excellent hot meals. For a while, we had the only hot food in the city, and other federal, state, and local agencies often came to visit about meal time, which greatly facilitated inter-agency cooperation. (USCG, Mike Howell)

served a very good meal prepared by nicely dressed people who were very polite and sometimes famous. It was a glimpse of normalcy in a world turned upside-down. It offered professional benefits as well. Since the Coast Guard had the only hot food in the area, members of other law enforcement and rescue agencies were soon regular visitors to the station. We were happy to share our good fortune, and strong relationships were established at the working level between our Coasties and the local officers from the FBI, U.S. Customs, the DEA, the Louisiana State Police, and many others who helped the overall rescue operation in many ways. The food was great, but it was more than that; it was a bit of civilization, a reminder of how great America is and why everybody was working so hard. I could not have asked for better food, a better morale booster, or a better networking situation, yet it was exactly what we needed. The Lord was providing.

By now the RVs and trailers that Sector and district

A travel trailer parked beside the PGA mess tent. (USCG, Mike Howell)

headquarters had ordered had begun to arrive. The tent city gradually decreased in size as crews were moved into more civilized accommodations. CWO Dan Brooks handled it all with a minimum of fuss, arranging parking sites, assembling electrical hookups, and managing a host of issues bound to come up when turning a tent city into a trailer park, all while rescuing thousands of people. Portable toilets were an important issue as well. The temporary Sector headquarters in Alexandria was doing an amazing job of sending supplies and equipment, including temporary restrooms, to the station. But getting the portable toilets emptied was impossible; there were no service operators functioning in the New Orleans area. The only solution was to keep sending down more portable toilets. At one point we had over fifty of them lined up, mostly full, and then the vice president of the United States came to visit.

We were almost overrun with distinguished visitors. Many senators, congressmen, and various Cabinet-level personnel wanted to witness the disaster that was New Orleans. This was a good thing; they needed to understand what had happened in New Orleans and how the rescue operation was going. The people who made all the decisions in Washington needed some firsthand knowledge. Usually they arrived full of TV knowledge, knowing everything there was to know about the storm and the city. Then we took them up in a helicopter for an overview and they were stunned into silence. It is one thing to measure the disaster through a television screen, but that is like looking through a straw. When they were up in the helicopter, everywhere they looked was flooded, and the sky was full of helicopters, orange ones, black ones, and white ones, all hovering and hoisting. When they looked down they could see many small boats running down the streets, rescuing people, and that was reality, harsh and stark in every respect. They were usually pretty quiet when we landed. Thankfully, they always asked what they could do to help. To be fair, everybody who first arrived was like that, including the incoming Coasties, knowing it all and full of ideas. But they got a reality check once they realized the magnitude of the disaster. Only then did they become useful for the operation.

I received a call from the Secret Service that Vice President Dick Cheney would be visiting. With rescues in full swing, we couldn't do much in the way of preparation, and I figured the vice president should see things as they really were. During normal military operations, a visit by a dignitary such as the vice president would generate a flurry of preparations, painting or polishing everything that didn't move and some things that did. But in this case, he would see us as we were, working very hard to save lives.

At this point in our rescue operations, National Guard helicopters were flying very low over the station every few minutes, carrying Super Sacks full of thousands of pounds

Army and National Guard helicopters carried Super Sacks of fill material from a point beside Station New Orleans to fill the breech in the 17th Street Canal levee. Many of the helicopters passed directly over the station, preventing any conversation as the loud helicopters flew over, often every three or four minutes. (USCG, Mike Howell)

of sand and rock to fill the breach in the 17th Street Canal. They were staging from a point of land extending into the lake right next to the station. The noise was horrendous, but we quickly got used to it, pausing in mid-conversation as a helicopter went by, then resuming our conversation once the noise had decreased. For Mike Howell, it was like Vietnam all over again. Helicopters were everywhere, and he was tickled pink. He was moving and shaking with his camera, happy and snapping away. With all this aerial traffic, it was hard to tell which helicopter carried our distinguished visitors. Eventually, what was obviously a visiting helicopter arrived, carrying Secret Service agents and Alberto Gonzales, the Attorney General of the United States.

The vice president's arrival was delayed, so I escorted Mr. Gonzales to my office. I must admit that after spending a career in law enforcement, it was cool to be visiting and making small talk with the Attorney General of the United States. My impression was that he was a good guy and genuinely wanted to help in any way he could. We enjoyed a pleasant conversation, and then I remembered something he really could help me with. By this time FEMA was getting irritated that the PGA was feeding us. They had demanded we shut down their meal service because the PGA wasn't on a government contract, which was true. FEMA declared that they couldn't ensure the quality of the food, and therefore we might be getting substandard rations, which was certainly not true. I explained all of this to Mr. Gonzales and asked if he, as the attorney general, would permit the PGA to supply our food. Mr. Gonzales smiled and gave me permission to keep the PGA cooking for us, and to use his name as my authority. I did, and it worked very well for another two weeks, during which time we enjoyed seriously good food prepared by an exceptionally kind group of professionals. Eventually the FEMA legal machine kicked in, and with lawyers calling me repeatedly, we had to let the PGA go, but it was wonderful while it lasted.

When the vice president arrived, he looked around the station and asked a lot of questions about the operation. He spent a lot of time shaking hands and encouraging everybody. The crew, by this time a collection of Coasties from all over the nation, was thrilled. Junior enlisted men and women can tell in a heartbeat if a leader cares about them or not, and they could tell Vice President Cheney was truly concerned about what they were doing and, more importantly, how they were doing. It felt good. Then he wanted to see the breach in the 17th Street Canal, and I was a bit concerned. It was about 98 degrees and there wasn't a breath of wind. And it was humid, very humid. I knew from the news over the last couple of years that the vice president had a history of heart issues,

Vice President Dick Cheney visited Station New Orleans and received a briefing from myself and Lieutenant Commander Sean Regan. I found the vice president to be amazingly sharp, with an excellent grasp of the realities of our situation and quite supportive of our efforts.

I wore a Station Grand Isle cap because at that time there were no Sector New Orleans hats available for commanders and captains. Since Station Grand Isle was wiped out operationally and their Coasties were doing rescues all over the city, I wore their hat with pride to honor them. (USCG, Mike Howell)

and he was a stocky man. It was a good walk from the station to the bridge overlooking the large hole in the 17th Street Canal, where he could get a clear view of the flooded Lakeview neighborhood, and I was worried. I was sure it was going to be a great photo op, since he came with a full entourage of various news camera crews. As a Coast Guard officer, I was trained to anticipate problems, and in the back of my mind, I feared the vice president would have a heart attack, live on FOX News and CNN, standing next to me on the bridge overlooking the flooded city. But Mr. Cheney wasn't easily deterred. I made sure our medical corpsman accompanied us, and with Mrs. Cheney clearly watching her husband from a polite distance, we headed out to the levee breach. Our guests were all sweating profusely by the time we reached the bridge. They were totally soaked, but we all made it there and back without incident. I was greatly relieved. The vice president, the rescue operation, and my career were all intact.

As the visit was drawing to a close, the Vice President of the United States said he needed to use the restroom. I was mortified. I had nothing decent to offer him. I tried to convince him to delay, but that was not to be. We had a long line of portable toilets, about three-fourths of which were full and thus no longer in use. Normally the smell of so many full johns would have been horrendous, but frankly the waters we were operating in were full of sewage and a host of other pollutants, so the smell of the johns blended in with the smell of everything else. I was still hugely embarrassed. I directed him to one of the less full johns, and thankfully, the camera crews showed discretion and didn't film the event.

Outside the portable toilets, we had set up sanitation stations with containers of hand sanitizer. The rule was that every single person had to use the sanitation station after leaving the john. We were very worried about disease, and this was just one of the measures we enforced to protect ourselves. When the vice president came out, he smiled— sort of—but clearly was not particularly happy. I doubt the vice president had used a portable toilet in quite a while. As he walked toward his wife and staff, I intercepted him and pointed him toward the sanitation station to clean up. He started to protest, and I put on the full captain face and directed him politely but firmly. It was important. Every member of the crew was watching, and if I let him get away with it, they would feel they could be exempt too. Mr. Cheney was gracious and complied.

Before he left I shook his hand farewell and thanked him

profusely for his visit. He thanked everybody for all the good work they were doing, and he took off in his helicopter. It is a humorous anecdote, and yet it shows what a kind and humble man Vice President Cheney is. He could have made a stink at being ordered around by a mere captain in the Coast Guard, but he graciously complied. He deeply impressed me, and later when the press was unkind toward him, I found myself bristling. By my own experience, he was a very good man.

You Didn't Bring Enough for Everybody

On Day Four after the storm, things were slowly starting to get organized. New Orleans International Airport had become both a hospital and an evacuation center. This vital link to the outside world was not reclaimed easily. Roads had to be cleared around the airport, runways had to be cleared of debris, emergency power had to be set up, and beds and medical personnel brought in. Enough people had been rescued that there was now a need to move them from their temporary shelters and evacuate them to locations outside the city. This need became more pressing as each day passed.

Obviously, getting people out of the water was always the first priority. And once the boat crews got the victims to dry land, others moved them to safer locations. During the first couple of days Coasties performed both legs of the operation, but as time progressed, the responsibility of moving these exhausted and bedraggled people was often handed off to the National Guard or local police and sheriff's deputies. Sometimes this resulted in a double counting of rescues, with the Coasties counting a rescue as moving a person from a flooded house to dry land, often staging areas on higher ground such as train tracks, and the next agency counting a rescue as moving a person from train tracks to a civilized rescue center. But what mattered was that people were getting rescued in ever increasing numbers. And now, on Day Four, enough people had been rescued to require that they be moved to the airport for further evacuation.

Petty Officer Eric Douglas had been given the difficult assignment of organizing a large number of recent rescues into

A Coastie from the cutter Spencer *helps Katrina survivors onto a bus headed out of the city. (USCG, Mike Tippets)*

small groups so that they could be bused to the airport. This turned out to be a tough duty. These people had been through a lot. They had lost their homes and everything they owned to the floodwaters. All of their things were ruined: clothes, papers, furniture, food, and, worst of all, photographs that could never be replaced. And these people were exhausted. Sleep was nearly impossible with the temperatures in the high 90s every day. The humidity hovering near ninety percent made it feel even hotter. They were hungry and thirsty, and many were definitely angry. They were furious at what had happened to them. Some wanted to blame someone else for their decision to stay and ride out the storm; some thought the government should have evacuated them before the storm; others were just angry in general. When you lose everything you have and you're isolated from family and friends and the world as you know it has been turned upside-down, such feelings are pretty normal, as far as anything is normal in such a mess.

Eric Douglas was a Boatswain's Mate, Third Class, meaning he was trained in driving rescue boats in very bad weather on oceans and lakes. He wasn't trained in crowd control, yet this is where he found himself. There was simply no one else to do the job. The crowd was large, and they were getting rowdy waiting for the overdue buses to arrive. Frankly, just getting buses moving took a lot of coordination in a city where almost every street was blocked with downed poles and power lines, trees, houses, and debris cluttering and blocking the way. Someone had to find fuel for the buses, find keys for the buses, and find drivers willing to drive them. Then there had to be a safe place for the buses to transport the people, where food and water would be available, before loading the survivors onto further transportation out of the area. All told, it required significant logistics to get buses to these newly rescued people. But the hungry, hot, exhausted crowd didn't know all that. All they knew was that they were miserable and the buses were late. In a city where buses always ran on time and were quite regular, the fact that these buses were behind schedule was simply another insult on top of all they had endured. No one among them seemed to realize that just getting a couple of buses moving on their behalf was a major undertaking.

So they were tired, hungry, thirsty, and angry. Those who could find alcohol were drunk, and undoubtedly a few were high. One intoxicated woman was very angry and stirred up the other people waiting for the buses. She was very vocal in her complaints, the same complaints everybody else had, but she was insistent, persistent, and quite loud. She was starting to have an effect on the crowd and it wasn't good. When the buses finally arrived, one of the requirements for boarding the bus was to throw away all alcohol and drugs, for the safety of everyone being transported. This woman refused to give up her bottle and became even more agitated, loudly challenging the authority of the Coasties in general and Petty Officer Douglas in particular. A riot was in the making. Thinking quickly, Douglas approached the lady. The crowd immediately settled down and became quiet so they could hear as well as see what would transpire. It promised to be interesting. Petty Officer Douglas, a very young man, quietly explained to the inebriated woman that since she didn't bring enough for everybody, she would have to part with the bottle. In a strange way, this made sense to her, for natives of New Orleans are hospitable people, freely sharing what they have at any party or public gathering. So with more than fifty other evacuees closely watching, she quietly gave up her bottle and boarded the bus. The tense situation was defused, the buses were boarded, and the people were taken to the airport, given hot food, medical attention, and evacuation to a better place than their beloved but flooded city.

Many people outside the city criticized the way things were progressing. But inside the effort, hundreds of people were making very good decisions under horrible conditions, doing their best, and sometimes doing beyond the best that could be done. What people fail to realize is that we lost a major city when Katrina hit New Orleans. Fortunately, thankfully, most of the population was spared by the highly effective evacuation, but the storm took out everything that makes civilization work. Almost all at once it was like living in 1850 again, surviving without electricity, running water, an effective police force, fire department, or basic city services. Worse than that, New Orleans was the center of the metropolitan area and the region. Before the storm, when you needed something in the surrounding cities and suburbs and you couldn't get it, you could always find it in New Orleans. Every service or industry was based either in New Orleans or adjoining Jefferson Parish. Most major services ran either out of or through New Orleans. For example, some people in the Florida panhandle, three states away, lost their internet service because the system was based in New Orleans. And Mississippi, Alabama, Georgia, and much of Florida had fuel shortages because the oil refineries in New Orleans along the Mississippi River were closed.

With New Orleans on her knees, the surrounding areas were seriously crippled too. If a major U.S. city were to be hit with a sudden disaster, say a small nuclear bomb, one that took out the electricity, water, gas, police force, fire department, city services, and government, the results would be catastrophic. That is what New Orleans was facing. A massive epidemic could cause similar problems, as would an electromagnetic pulse attack, which would wipe out everything electrical and electronic. For disaster response planning, Katrina has become the model, and it has been studied by disaster preparedness planners around the world. After the storm response was complete, planners from France came to interview the Coasties who led the operation in order to capture the lessons learned for their own possible future disaster situations. The only advantage New Orleans had was that most of its population had evacuated. Given this complete breakdown of civilized society, recovery in New Orleans went remarkably smoothly.

For the newly rescued people boarding the buses, all they knew was that they were headed for safety. That was a good thing, and the result of the efforts of many resourceful people. The can-do attitude and ingenuity of Petty Officer Eric Douglas was typical of the Coast Guard men and women working in the miracle that was the rescue operation in New Orleans.

Douglas later volunteered to ride shotgun, literally, and provide security for ambulances driving a gauntlet of gunfire through very dangerous areas to reach the airport. Without his efforts and those of the other Coasties who volunteered for that hazardous duty, the ambulance drivers would not attempt the route, and many seriously injured people would have certainly died. Such selfless devotion to duty by the very youngest members of the service was an inspiration to us all. That all their critically injured and wounded passengers, as well as the drivers and guardians themselves, came through without a scratch shows the Lord was protecting this desperate mission.

On the River

Operations on the Mississippi River started before the storm, with the Coast Guard cutter *Pamlico* leading a convoy of eight 41-footers and three 55-footers up the river to Baton Rouge to ride out the storm. The 41-footers were general-purpose aluminum rescue boats with twin inboard diesel engines, and at thirty-five tons, they were far too large to trailer. In 2005, the 41-footer was the Coast Guard's core rescue boat. They were very capable boats designed to be deployed in terrible weather conditions and rescue mariners in distress at sea. However, these boats were built in the early 1970s and were now more than thirty years old—thirty years spent getting hammered in terrible weather conditions that sank other vessels, thirty years spent conducting thousands of operations and patrols. Even with very dedicated maintenance and repair, they were showing their age. Aluminum gets brittle as it ages, and the joke was that their aluminum hulls would crack if you looked at them wrong, and sometimes it seemed to be true.

The 41-footers, two each from Station New Orleans, Station Grand Isle, Station Venice, and Station Gulfport, went with three 55-foot aids to navigation boats from teams based in Dulac, Venice, and New Orleans. All three teams would be homeless for quite some time as their bases were severely flooded or destroyed by Hurricane Katrina or Hurricane Rita, which followed a month later. The 55-footers are sturdy boats, designed to stay out for days, with galley and berthing facilities onboard so the crew can eat and sleep. But these boats were built in the 1960s and thus were even older than the 41-footers. In the civilian world, we would never use a thirty-five- or forty-year-old car as our daily driver for commuting to work, yet these were the tools we gave our young men and women to rescue mariners in desperate conditions in the open ocean.

The mothership of this operation was the *Pamlico*, a 160-foot construction tender. *Pamlico* was designed to build the structures of the major navigational aids used by large ships transiting major waterways like the Mississippi River. These structures are often constructed with several long piles, like telephone poles, driven deep into the riverbed and wired together with thick steel cables. Once this base is constructed, the appropriate color board and lights are installed, along with batteries for the lights and solar panels for the batteries. Since these structures don't move in normal operations, the

Coast Guard 41-foot rescue boats tied up alongside Pamlico *for evacuation. (USCG)*

ship pilots rely on them when they navigate the large ships up and down the river. With a large crane up forward, fabrication and repair facilities down below, and an innovation mindset, *Pamlico*'s crew was well suited for the task soon to be at hand. Like the small boats she was escorting, *Pamlico* had more than three decades of hard service behind her. For the eleven small boats in the convoy, the good news was that together they had enough spare parts, several highly skilled mechanics, and the *Pamlico*'s equipment to fix things as they broke and keep all the boats underway.

Once the storm had passed, the little convoy made their way downriver to New Orleans. As with every Coast Guard operation in and around the city, they had to take with them everything they would need for several days; it would be a

The galley on Pamlico *where the meals were prepared for not only* Pamlico's *crew, but also the crews of the five 41-footers and the three 55-foot aids to navigation boats tied up with* Pamlico. *(USCG, Mike Howell)*

while before they could be resupplied. They had to proceed very carefully, as Katrina had cut a wide swath, and the water was rife with trees, parts of houses, and equipment from the many facilities that line the river. Add to this the damaged and sunken barges, and even a car or two, and the trip was fraught with danger. Once they reached Kenner Bend Anchorage, at the western end of the city, things got a lot worse. Large ships had dragged their anchors in the 130-mile-per-hour winds and were now pushed up on the batture, that portion of land on the river side of the levee. Getting these ships back to deep water would prove to be a challenge. There was one large ship precariously anchored next to the Nashville Avenue wharf that was dangerously close to hitting the wharf. Car ferries had washed aground on the batture, and one large ship had broken free from the anchorage and crushed two towboats on the west bank of the river. It was a dangerous and careful journey, but they made it with haste. They knew people were dying in New Orleans and they were needed to save lives.

Chief Warrent Officer Robert Lewald was Commanding Officer on the cutter *Pamlico* during the Katrina operation. With over two decades of experience in all things connected with boats, Lewald had risen through the enlisted ranks to become a Chief Warrant Officer, Boatswain's Mate. Attaining this rank takes a tremendous amount of hard work and dedication and shows clearly both his technical expertise and his leadership. A soft-spoken man, this highly effective leader was loved and respected by his crew, and his calm leadership was to be an anchor to the highly effective river rescue operation.

Upon arriving in New Orleans, Lewald's convoy found the destruction to be both impressive and depressing. It soon became obvious that Chalmette Slip, downriver from New Orleans' badly flooded Lower Ninth Ward and south of the city, had become a gathering place for people forced out of their homes by the flood in Chalmette. Chalmette Slip is a berthing area cut into the bank of the river at an angle, with a dock on both sides for small and medium-sized ships. Before the storm arrived it was seen as a safe haven, a hurricane hole, for towboats, crew boats, and other craft that could fit there, even a floating grain elevator. After the storm, the high ground of Chalmette Slip was some of the only land on the east bank of the river in St. Bernard Parish that was not submerged. Hundreds and then thousands of people gathered there, leaving behind homes devastated by flooding and often oiled by the huge oil tanks that ruptured at the nearby Murphy Oil Refinery.

Before Katrina, Chalmette was a community of extended families. Everybody knew each other, and children could play outside under the watchful eye of relatives and neighbors.

A ruptured oil tank at the Murphy Oil Refinery spread a layer of oil over the already devastating floodwaters that engulfed Chalmette. (USCG)

Even a decade after Katrina ravaged the city, the people who once lived there talk about how wonderful it was, and those who have stayed to rebuild are determined to re-create the family-friendly, hardworking town they all loved. With the devastation from the oil on top of the destruction from the flood, bringing Chalmette back to its former self has been hard, and many haven't returned. They couldn't take the risk of losing everything again if the levees built by the Army Corps of Engineers should fail once more in the next big storm. In some cases, claims are still being settled more than ten years after Katrina. In the immediate aftermath of the storm, however, the people gathering in Chalmette Slip were in a state of shock. They had just lost everything in an unbelievable flood they were assured could never happen.

Chief Warrant Officer Lewald and his team got to work, and though the job was massive, he had help from a variety of sources. Along with the *Pamlico* and its convoy of 41-footers and 55-footers, the cutters *Clamp* and *Greenbrier* were soon in the mix. With support from local police and sheriff's offices, Louisiana Wildlife and Fisheries, and the Louisiana Department of Transportation, the rescuers got busy. The twelve Coast Guard cutters and boats were soon ferrying people from Chalmette Slip to the ferry landing in New Orleans. Even as they were joined by the city's ferry boats and other vessels on the river, including a couple of towboats, people were arriving at Chalmette Slip faster than they could be transported away. A better solution was needed.

Creativity and cooperation are two things in abundance in the New Orleans maritime community. With so much of the nation's commerce traveling up and down this nautical superhighway, the river system of commerce on the Mississippi River is incredibly effective and efficient, but it depends on every part working smoothly. A backup at one facility could mean a delay in loading or unloading several ships, which would mean they would fill spots in the anchorages that could be assigned to other ships. In turn, this could delay still other ships from entering the river, all costing their owners tens of thousands of dollars a day or more in food and fuel charges per ship, not to mention lost cargo charges, which can quickly mount into the hundreds of thousands of dollars. Likewise, any delays impacting barges, with tens of thousands of tons of cargo needing to be loaded or unloaded, will cause serious problems among the barge fleets. This causes the towboats that push the hundreds of barges up and down the river to be held up or rerouted to account for the delays. These delays also mean cargo does not reach its destination on time. Gasoline may not make it from the refinery to Florida as scheduled; grain elevators in St. Louis are overloaded; power plants run low on fuel; or fertilizer doesn't make it to the farmer in Nebraska. All of these delays are expensive, and the ripples of a major delay can be felt for a long time. In this port environment, involving hundreds of large ships, tens of thousands of barges, and millions of tons of cargo every year, all companies and agencies on the river have developed a cooperative competition. Sure the companies and even industries compete with each other, but they all know they also have to rely on each other and all have to make sure the system works for the good of all.

In this highly cooperative environment, a good answer to the problem of moving large numbers of people from Chalmette Slip soon appeared. The towboat *Blackbeard*, from Turn Services, was pressed into service, along with the deck barge it was pushing from Associated Terminals. Barges come in three basic varieties: liquid barges for carrying fuels and chemicals; hopper barges, which have huge holds for carrying dry cargo such as grain, fertilizer, and coal; and deck barges, which are flat and can carry rock, large cargo cranes, pipes, and anything else that can be strapped down. *Blackbeard*, an 1,800-horsepower, 65-foot towing vessel, was faced up to a 250-foot deck barge, meaning she was securely attached to it with thick steel wires, which is how towboats typically push barges on the river. Like a number of smaller vessels,

Blackbeard had ridden out the storm in Chalmette Slip, and Captain Joseph Kieffer quickly responded to the Coast Guard request for help. *Blackbeard* and her deck barge could carry between three hundred and four hundred people at a time as she ferried people out of Chalmette. A photo of *Blackbeard* and her deck barge, loaded with a couple hundred displaced people in life jackets, made national news and demonstrated the excellent cooperation between Coast Guard and private companies in the Katrina rescue and recovery. In this one operation, well over seven thousand people trapped in St. Bernard were rescued.

The people now being transported to safety, like most survivors in New Orleans, had been through a lot, and the future looked pretty bleak for them all. Their houses were destroyed along with everything they owned. They weren't sure if beloved family members were alive, dead, or, even

The Coast Guard received help from Turn Services, which used its towboat Blackbeard *and an Associated Terminals deck barge to move thousands of people from the flooded areas of Chalmette. (USCG)*

worse, somewhere out there in the flooded mess, barely hanging on to life and hoping, praying to be found. Many of them had large extended families living in Chalmette, which made the uncertainty almost unbearable. Many worked in the Chalmette area, and they could clearly see that, like their homes, their jobs, the source of income to support their families, had disappeared under the floodwaters. While the larger industries like the oil refinery might resume service someday, even those companies wouldn't be handing out paychecks for a very long time.

Some people were injured and needed urgent medical attention. Ms. Cindy Fourman, a nurse from Charity Hospital, probably saved over 250 lives as she treated the survivors transferred by the boats. Boatswain's Mate Second Class Emily Ernst served as an emergency medical technician and provided first aid to thousands of people, both an exhausting and a rewarding job. Boatswain's Mate Third Class William Kupfer worked in several locations during the rescue effort, but he spent a lot of time working the Chalmette rescue. He gave first aid to hundreds of people, including two gunshot victims who were peppered with buckshot, a lady suffering from seizures and severe breathing problems, and a young man who had recently received a kidney transplant. He also performed first aid on five babies that had to be evacuated by helicopter due to their serious condition. During his most notable medical emergency, a frantic and desperate father brought a baby to him who had stopped breathing and was turning blue. Kupfer immediately and very gently began first aid, breathing life into the little body. After what seemed like forever to both Kupfer and the father, but was probably only a matter of moments, the baby responded and started breathing on its own. Seeing that the baby was overheated, Kupfer did his best to cool down the infant and then arranged for the child's medevac by helicopter.

Petty Officers Eric Gonzalez and Richard Forte shifted to the river operation after working in the flood punts and

Coasties helping people from Chalmette off the barge to safety. (USCG)

rescuing hundreds there. Given this new assignment, they made their way to the Algiers ferry landing, where they helped offload the thousands of people being ferried from Chalmette, sometimes carrying the injured on stretchers from the boat, up the landing, and to the top of the levee. Gonzalez, a Boatswain's Mate First Class, and Forte, a Marine Science Technician Second Class, provided basic first aid, food, water, security, and comfort to the growing masses as they awaited further transportation to shelters.

Unfortunately, around 5:00 PM, the buses shuttling people out of New Orleans stopped arriving at the ferry terminal. This left about two thousand individuals stranded without shelter for the night. These people had just been through their own personal vision of hell on earth, and when they realized they might be stuck on the levee for the night, they became increasingly angry. Convinced the crowd would begin to riot and many of the injured would not survive if left on their own overnight, Gonzales and Forte banded together with three other Coasties, six sheriff's deputies from Calcasieu Parish, and two New Orleans police officers to provide security for the remaining evacuees and locate transportation for them. Though outnumbered two thousand to eleven, they managed to calm the volatile situation while they worked for a solution. Showing both tremendous initiative and an outstanding grasp of what needed to be done in the face of sheer chaos among the evacuees, they managed to commandeer twenty buses from two different locations. At a time when bus transportation was the single hardest support asset to obtain in the city and every agency and group in the state was working feverishly to try to locate buses, this was an amazing achievement. Demonstrating remarkable leadership, Gonzalez and Forte worked until almost midnight to load the last of that day's remaining evacuees onto buses and send them to safety in Baton Rouge.

While its citizens faced the harsh realities of life after destruction, local governments on the badly flooded east bank of the river, particularly in St. Bernard Parish and Plaquemines Parish, struggled to carry out even the most basic administration. With a few exceptions, everything in St. Bernard was under ten to twenty feet of water. Offices, equipment, telephones, computers, desks, files, staplers, everything needed to run any sort of operation, were all submerged, unavailable, or destroyed. And yet civil order had to be restored. Officials needed a place to work and a place to sleep as they tried to piece things together for their friends, relatives, and constituents. In this desperate situation, the Coast Guard worked with MARAD, the Maritime Administration, to provide a solution in the form of the USNS *Shreveport* and the cruise ship *Scotia Prince*.

These ships were available for local use, but they were not yet in New Orleans, and getting them up from the Gulf of Mexico through a hundred miles of twisting river would be difficult. The river was closed and had been since the Sunday afternoon before Katrina struck. While the Coast Guard had shut down the river in an orderly fashion, making sure everything was properly closed up and secure and the ships left in the river were properly moored or anchored, things certainly weren't orderly after Katrina came through. Although the massive amount of debris in the river and along the levee looked terrible from the air, the unseen obstacles under the water's surface were the real problems with moving a large ship on the river. If a large ship such as the *Shreveport* or *Scotia Prince* hit a sunken vessel, the impact would literally tear a hole in the moving ship, causing it to take on massive amounts of water and possibly sink, potentially blocking the river for weeks and even months. With each day the river was closed costing about $400 million dollars, the risk of sinking such a major ship in the river was a national-level risk, one that could seriously cripple the entire nation's economy. There aren't enough rail cars or semitrailer trucks on the entire North American continent to even begin to handle the cargo moved daily should the Mississippi River be blocked.

And the risk was great. While all major ships were accounted for in the New Orleans area, barges were a big concern, and downriver there were barges scattered all over the river and the levee.

While most barge and fleeting companies had properly secured their barges and fleets, one obviously had not, and the result was a large number of barges sunk in the shallows of the river. Some were grounded on the batture; some were perched on top of the levee; others found themselves on the wrong side of the levee; and an unknown number were sunk in the river. A barge fleet serves as a parking lot of sorts for large numbers of barges waiting to load or unload, where the barges are typically secured to each other with large steel wires. These same steel cables secure tiers of barges, up to eight barges across, against large steel pipes called dolphins driven deep into the river. These are further secured with heavy steel wires shackled to thick chain, itself shackled to eight-thousand- or ten-thousand-pound anchors buried deep in the ground along the shore. Under normal conditions, these fleets rarely have barges break loose. For a hurricane, the steel wires holding the barges together are typically doubled up, with twice the number of wires holding them together, and this is sufficient for securing the barges.

The typical hopper, or open cargo, barge is a 195-foot-long floating cargo box, or a small ship without an engine. Barges are an amazingly efficient way to move cargo on the river. A barge can be loaded and then combined with other barges to form a large tow, sometimes up to forty-four barges with a total length of about fifteen hundred feet, equivalent to five football fields. This massive tow is pushed by one towboat and one crew and moves the equivalent weight capacity of seven hundred rail cars or twenty-six hundred tractor-trailer trucks within a single tow. A towboat moving up or down the river can drop various barges off at different facilities, depending on the cargo and its destination, all while keeping the tow moving. Without question, this is the most fuel efficient and people efficient way to move cargo in the nation, and though they most certainly are, most towboat captains don't think of themselves as being in an environmentally friendly or very green industry. But now the problem was that nobody knew if there were barges sunk in the main shipping channel of the river. If so, these long steel boxes could sink any ship that hit them.

The National Oceanographic and Atmospheric Administration had relocated to Alexandria with the Coast Guard Sector and were advising Captain Frank Paskewich. They provided boats with underwater side-scanning sonar in an attempt to find sunken barges in the river, and we had high hopes this would work. The boats did provide a good sonar map of the bottom of the river, but unfortunately the resolution was such that we couldn't be sure there weren't barges sunk in the shipping channel that the sonar map didn't show. This was a critical problem, for while the river looks wide, the actual shipping channel is often rather narrow. Were a barge or even a towboat to be sunk in this narrow channel, a ship could not pass without hitting it and ripping a hole in the ship. Were the ship to sink in the channel, it would take a massive salvage operation to move the hulk and clear the channel.

The other major problem with moving the USNS *Shreveport* and the *Scotia Prince* up the river was the missing navigational aids along the banks of the river. The navigation aids usually consist of dayboards, green square-shaped or red triangle-shaped boards for daylight navigation, and similarly colored lights for night navigation, both mounted on top of a pole driven into the ground at a specific point along the river. Floating aids are called buoys and are also red and green. For a ship entering a harbor or coming upriver, the rule is "red right returning," meaning keep the red buoys on the right side of the ship to stay in the channel and the green buoys on the left side of the ship. It is the opposite for a ship leaving a harbor or going downriver. The buoys were mostly washed away after the storm, but the real problem was the missing dayboards ashore, specifically the ranges. A range is two dayboards in a line, located some distance apart and lined up very precisely with a certain stretch of the channel. A range is located so that if the pilot on the ship can see the two dayboards lined up exactly, he knows the ship is safely in the channel. If one dayboard is to the left or right of the other even slightly, the pilot knows his ship is outside the channel and in great danger of running aground. With all the twists and turns of the Mississippi River, having the dayboards and ranges in place is absolutely essential to keeping a large ship in the channel. And after Katrina blasted through the area, passing directly over the lower part of the river, most of the dayboards were gone.

But the *Shreveport* and *Scotia Prince* were badly needed in New Orleans, and other large Navy ships were headed to the mouth of the Mississippi River as well, all waiting to come up the river to New Orleans to provide housing and offices for the beleaguered first responders and ravaged local governments. Captain Frank Paskewich had a decision to make, one with national-level consequences, and it was his alone to make. The channel might be clear, or it may have barges lurking at the bottom. The navigation aids were gone. The ship pilots, led by Captain Mike Lorino and Captain AJ Gibbs were willing to try. Ship pilots are highly experienced mariners who have memorized the entire stretch of river for which they are responsible, in this case from the mouth of the river to New Orleans, about 100 miles away. They undergo an intense training program teaching them to handle every kind of ship and memorize every aid to navigation they have to depend upon to safely navigate the vessel. But with the aids missing, it was like running an obstacle course in the dark, in the rain, without shoes. Even the slightest miscalculation could seriously damage a ship or even sink it. Think stubbing your toe, very hard, on a log you can't see or slicing your foot on sharp rocks under what looks like soft mud, and you have an idea of what the pilots faced, except on a much grander scale and with terrible consequences. Authorized by Captain Paskewich, the river pilots set out. Against all odds, they got the ships safely to New Orleans.

The *Shreveport* docked at the lower berth at Chalmette Slip, where FEMA planned to dock the *Scotia Prince*. FEMA wouldn't allow the cruise ship to come upriver without FEMA-qualified dock inspectors to inspect the docks after the storm. Fortunately, Lieutenant Commander Jimmy Duckworth was present to inspect the docks and found them safe. Though he wasn't FEMA qualified, the officials accepted his assessment and he ran teams of St. Bernard police officers to handle the lines from the ship while it tied up. Captain Lorino moved the *Scotia Prince* upriver while Captain Gibbs moved the *Shreveport* to the AMSTAR docks. By sunrise the *Scotia Prince* was in place, and by 9:00 that morning, the St. Bernard Parish president was onboard with his parish council, and they began the heavy lifting of bringing their flooded and shattered parish back to life.

On the Island, or Not

Station Grand Isle, on the Gulf Coast about fifty miles due south of New Orleans, was also severely flooded. The station building is built on the high ground, about seven feet above sea level, which is absolutely the high ground for about twenty miles in any direction. Once the headquarters of the pirates Jean Lafitte and his older brother Pierre, the island is now famous for its fishing. Station Grand Isle, like Stations Venice and Gulfport, works primarily rescues and fisheries enforcement, ensuring that enough breeding-age game fish remain to produce the next generation of fish. Individually, fishermen don't like being limited on how much they can catch or being told when and where they can cast for their favorite fish. But many fishermen make their living on the water, and they understand how quickly mankind could wipe out fish populations.

Station Grand Isle was older than the other stations, and its buildings weren't on stilts. Flooding had occurred from time to time through the years and was expected. For Katrina, the wall of water rushed in from the Gulf, washed through the station buildings, and into the bay behind Grand Isle itself. The wall of water wasn't nearly as high as it was in Gulfport, since Grand Isle was on the west side, or "safer" side, of the hurricane, but it still ravaged everything on the island and washed away the only bridge connecting the island to the mainland. The wave also wiped out the houses of the Coasties stationed there. The buildings stood, but roofs were severely damaged and in some cases carried away by the storm surge.

181

Coast Guard Station Grand Isle was operationally destroyed by the wall of water that came from the Gulf of Mexico and washed across the island. Pictured is the start of the slow rebuilding process. Everything had to be removed from each office building, maintenance building, and home. Rebuilding would take two years, during which time the station remained fully operational, conducting fisheries enforcement, drug enforcement, and search and rescue missions 24-7. (USCG, Rear Admiral Joseph Castillo)

Fortunately everyone was safe. All forty-one station personnel and their families, along with all six station rescue boats, were evacuated before the storm hit. Since Grand Isle, positioned as it is in the Gulf of Mexico, would be hit by the storm well before New Orleans would, the station had to be evacuated early. Complicating the evacuation was that the island only has one small bridge connecting it to the mainland, and once across this bridge, the two-lane road north to safety is only a couple of feet above sea level. This low road was extremely vulnerable to the rise in tide preceding any major storm, so the island had to be evacuated well before anybody else even worried about Katrina. It also meant the station was very good at evacuating, and Lieutenant Bill Gibbons' crew did a fine job securing the station and getting off the island.

Todd Harder was a Boatswain's Mate, First Class, meaning he was highly trained in all aspects of small boat operations. Being a first class, or BM1, meant he had been promoted five times, the last three as a specialized boatswain's mate, so he was highly experienced and a proven leader. As expected, the BM1 was a major player in getting all the Coasties, their families, and the rescue boats off the island before the storm. After the storm, there was no question of returning immediately to Grand Isle. The road was underwater for many miles, so Harder reported to Station New Orleans with his crew, Petty Officers Adam Lewis, Chris Herbert, and Travis Laza.

They arrived in time to help rid Station New Orleans of its looters and then got to work with rescues. With Station New Orleans personnel trying to bring their station back into operation, Harder coordinated with the National Guard and law enforcement to take into custody the sixty-three looters rounded up at the station. After dropping off the looters, Petty Officer Lewis worked with local fire department boats to evacuate elderly and infirm people to the Red Cross. One older gentleman rescued as part of this mission had been in his attic when he heard a boat drive near his house. He dove into the water and swam down through his flooded rooms to the second level of his home, where he kicked out a window to swim through. Badly lacerating his leg and ankle on the broken glass, he surfaced outside to be rescued by the passing boat and was taken to the station. With no medical supplies or personnel immediately available, Petty Officer Lewis put direct pressure on the wound, holding it tightly to stop the bleeding. While Lewis held the leg tightly, Petty Officer Harder ran back to the station for medical supplies, and the man's life was saved.

Station Grand Isle had a very shallow-draft 23-foot utility boat, not really a rescue boat in the traditional sense, but perfect for a flooded city, which is what Petty Officer Harder and his crew now faced. He launched the boat off a flooded bridge, surrounded by downed power lines and gas flares jetting up out of the water from broken gas lines. These gas flares could be quite dramatic, with flames at times rising many feet into the air. From a helicopter, it looked like parts of the flooded city were burning. During that first day of rescues, it was not uncommon to see a flooded house explode and then burn furiously when a spark set off a broken gas line.

During one rescue, the boat couldn't get close enough to the flooded and burning row of houses due to debris. While Petty Officer Herbert, who was the coxswain, positioned the boat as close as possible, Petty Officers Harder and Laza got out of the boat and waded through the severely contaminated water to pull a young woman from her submerged truck, saving her life. Next they heard noises coming from an office building, and they broke in to find two city workers trapped in the rafters. The men were panic-stricken. They had been driven into the rafters by rapidly rising water and had been without food and water. They had fully expected to die and now they were in shock. Even though rescue was at hand, the traumatized men wouldn't come down out of the rafters. Petty Officer Harder slowly talked the men down and got them to safety, and the team kept going. The Grand Isle crew, with Petty Officer Herbert maneuvering the boat carefully next to a partially submerged house, also rescued an elderly couple trapped upstairs. They were terrified and very grateful to be rescued. Their prayers had been answered.

Often the crew had to wade through water laced with human feces and unknown chemicals to make their rescues. But they went house to house, and in some cases roof to roof, to save those terrified and desperate people. This displaced rescue crew had no idea if their own homes on Grand Isle were wiped out, though witnessing the devastation in New

Orleans couldn't have left too much doubt about the fate of their island. Even so, they were undaunted and rescued nearly forty people that first day after the storm.

And the waters themselves got more interesting as time passed. Snakes had been driven out of their hiding places by the floods. Other animals were swimming too, but rats, cats, and others with legs and feet seemed to do better at quickly finding refuge. Here and there dead animals floated in the water. The floating balls of fire ants were a particularly nasty surprise. As their nests flooded, thousands of fire ants linked together in a large floating ball, which rotated a bit to allow the various ants to catch a breath from time to time. When the ball brushed up against something, the ants immediately rushed up onto the object, quite unpleasant if a rescue worker happened to be that something.

Petty Officer Harder and his team were one of the early Coast Guard teams to establish communications with the newly established emergency operations center at Zephyr Field, leading to the coordination of rescue operations in St. Bernard Parish. Later this would develop into the joint Coast Guard/FEMA Unified Command. These men, and the other early Coast Guard teams to arrive in New Orleans, were working fifteen-hour days in the boats. They were on the water as long as there was light to rescue. There were no showers, no washing machines, and they decontaminated with a bottle of water as best they could. Once somewhat cleaned up, they grabbed some cold food and slept when and where they could. There was no relief for them; they just kept working, operating with little regard for their personal safety.

When the road leading to Grand Isle became passable again, the crews began to head south to their home station. Though they were exhausted from their rescue operations in New Orleans, they now faced new challenges as their once beautiful station was devastated. The ground floors of the buildings had been washed through by waves of water, but the buildings stood, as they had been designed. The upper floors were full of mold, the natural result of everything being wet in such high temperatures. Piles of debris were everywhere. Offices and homes were ravaged; supplies were ruined by the water; all berthing and galley areas were destroyed. In short, little if anything could be used. This was made worse by the damage to the bridge connecting the island to the mainland and the distance of Grand Isle from the little towns on the road leading south, which were seriously impacted as well. It would be a slow recovery at Station Grand Isle. But the crew worked heroically, cleaning up the mess and setting things right while helping local citizens overcome their own personal disasters.

Office buildings can be refurbished or replaced and the mission goes on. But housing losses are personal and most of the Coasties living on Station Grand Isle lost everything. The Commanding Officer's house was a surreal mix of destruction and survival. The roof of the house was missing in some places and the damage inside the home was dramatic. His child's room still had soft pastel paint on the walls and the usual pictures and toys found in most children's rooms, but everything inside the room was wet and moldy, a total loss. Downstairs, everything was destroyed: upholstery, the kitchen table, carpets, paintings, walls, electronics, everything except a small china cabinet. This small cabinet holding his wife's grandmother's china seemed untouched. It was a minor miracle to be sure, but one greatly appreciated by a young Coastie wife who had just lost everything else she owned.

But the station recovered, like every Coast Guard unit damaged or destroyed by Katrina. It took some time, but as the rescues died down, RVs and camper trailers began arriving to house the crew and provide makeshift offices, and a food truck was sent to provide meals. The Integrated Support Command in Miami searched for contractors who could and would refurbish the station office buildings and houses. The ISC, as it was called, was extremely busy working

Rear Admiral Robert Duncan and Captain Joseph Castillo visited Station Grand Isle to get a first-hand briefing of conditions there. (USCG, Rear Admiral Joseph Castillo)

to get every Coast Guard unit in the New Orleans area rebuilt or restored. After the floodwaters receded, contractors would start streaming into New Orleans from the surrounding states to rebuild the city, but it was exceedingly difficult to find a contractor willing to drive past thousands of lucrative jobs to take a government repair contract on a little island at the end of a very long road. But ISC kept at it, and Bill Gibbons proved to be an exceptional officer during the interim. He kept morale high while he and his little band slowly rebuilt their station. It would take more than nine million dollars and over a year before the station was finished and the first families could move back into their houses.

It is to his credit, and that of his dedicated crew, that just over two years after Katrina, Station Grand Isle won the coveted Sumner I. Kimball Readiness Award for Coast Guard boat operations. This award is given to the top five percent of boat units in the Coast Guard, and for Station Grand Isle to earn this award only two years after being almost totally destroyed by the hurricane of the century is simple amazing.

Rescue from Above

This is primarily a book about the Coast Guard surface rescue in the aftermath of Hurricane Katrina, an operation that ultimately saved more than twenty-five thousand people by boat, usually one at a time and in miserable conditions. Surface operations was my world during the Katrina and later Rita operations, but I would be amiss and gravely negligent if I didn't highlight the amazingly brave Coast Guard pilots and aircrew who flew hundreds if not thousands of missions over the city and the amazing support system that kept the helicopters and airplanes in the air day after day. These Coast Guard aviators, who saved more than nine thousand people, mostly by helicopter hoist, will always be heroes.

Many of the helicopters were equipped with hoist cameras that filmed the hoist events. This was usually the footage of rescue operations that made it onto CNN or FOX News, usually very dramatic footage. By contrast, the boat forces had direct orders from the top not to let news cameras into the little boats. They didn't want pictures of dead bodies on the national news. It would have been most unfortunate if relatives thought they had seen the remains of a loved one broadcast on television. Though the no-camera policy kept the boat forces' heroic rescues out of the news and the national dialog, it undoubtedly saved great emotional pain for families across the nation.

Even before Katrina's winds had ceased, Coast Guard helicopters were daring the turbulent air over New Orleans, coming in behind the storm. Captain Bruce Jones had evacuated his aircraft from Air Station New Orleans to

Houston and Lake Charles. As the worst had passed, all five Air Station New Orleans helicopters arrived in Houma, Louisiana, by 2:00 PM that Monday in preparation to reenter the city. From there one took off to survey the mouth of the Mississippi River, one to Grand Isle to assess conditions there, and the rest to New Orleans. By 2:50, they had made the first helicopter rescue after the storm, hoisting two adults and a four-month-old infant from a small boat stuck in a tree near Port Sulphur, downriver of New Orleans. By the end of the day Air Station New Orleans helicopters had rescued 137 people, but there were many more to come.

The aviation community sprang into action and helicopters from the Aviation Training Center in Mobile, Alabama, soon arrived, as did helicopters from Texas Coast Guard bases. In time more than forty percent of the entire Coast Guard helicopter fleet were working the Katrina rescue, as well as many fixed-wing aircraft. This put a huge strain on the Coast Guard aviation community, as the aircraft left behind in their home units, from Miami to Alaska, still had to maintain their normal operations. In the case of Air Station Cape Cod, two helicopters from the Canadian Coast Guard flew to conduct operations at the Cape so that all the Coast Guard helicopters could fly to New Orleans to help. As the air rescue effort rapidly expanded, the Naval Air Station Joint Reserve Base in Belle Chasse, where the Coast Guard Air Station is located, would become one of the busiest air bases in the country, from which Coast Guard, National Guard, and military aircraft from every branch would operate.

When Air Station New Orleans crews first flew back into the city, they found their base seriously impacted, but they managed to return it to service. Runways had to be cleared, damaged hangers had to be repaired, and a number of very complex systems had to be made functional again. All this had to be done without electricity until the emergency generator systems could be brought on line. This alone was a big job, and took the efforts of many. An immediate problem those first few days was accessing the fuel in the fuel tanks stored underground. The fuel pumps wouldn't work, and it wasn't looking good for rescue operations. Helicopters are wonderful things, but they do drink the fuel. A typically resourceful Coastie, Petty Officer Gordon, rewired the Navy fuel farm to work with portable generators and got the system working again. His efforts enabled the most amazing helicopter rescue hoist operation in our history.

With the initial problems solved, Air Station New Orleans became the forward operating base for Coast Guard air in the New Orleans area. Captain Bruce Jones directed much of the Coast Guard helicopter fleet in daily operations. His team was superb, and they saved thousands of lives. But helicopters require serious maintenance; they have a *lot* of moving parts. Performing this intensive maintenance in New Orleans wasn't a good option, but the Coast Guard Aviation Training Center in Mobile, Alabama, was close by, at least by aircraft terms. Captain Dave Callahan at the Aviation Training Center took on both the maintenance and the crew rest and recovery roles for the New Orleans teams. The aircraft would fly to New Orleans and operate out of Air Station New Orleans all day conducting rescue operations; many would return to the Aviation Training Center at night. After a long day the exhausted crews could get a hot meal while a team of expert mechanics from all over the Coast Guard would perform the required maintenance and repair to the helicopters, often working all night, to ensure the birds were ready to fly and rescue the next morning. As every senior military officer knows, tactics and operations are important, but the key to success is logistics, and Captain Callahan's team had that working exceptionally well.

Even so, many of those helicopters were operating under marginal conditions. The HH-65s, the small orange helicopters, were all scheduled for transmission replacements, but the long-awaited start of the program wasn't to be until late in the year, well after the Katrina rescue operation.

Therefore, throughout the mission, their transmissions were weak, limiting the helicopter when working in the heat, and with temperatures in the high 90s in early September, this was a daily concern. In these conditions, the weight of the helicopter is absolutely critical. Whether the helicopter took off with a full load of fuel and some supplies or came back low on fuel but full of rescued people, the result was the same: a very heavy helicopter straining the transmission. And failure could be deadly. In most cases when I was in an HH-65, the pilots took off for the flight with the transmission warning lights reading yellow for danger or even red for serious danger. When I asked the pilots about those lights, they confirmed that the flashing warning lights meant the flight was not a good idea. But the pilots pressed on bravely, knowing they were flying beyond the limits of safety to rescue

The smaller HH-65 Dauphin was the workhorse of the Coast Guard rescue operation, as they are the bulk of the Coast Guard helicopter fleet. (USCG)

people who desperately needed it. Some told me the Lord was with them. It would seem to have been so.

The very nature of the rescue mission also unduly taxed the helicopters. Hovering the helicopter, remaining stationary over a specific place, was essential to hoisting survivors from the disaster below. Unfortunately, hovering puts the most strain on a helicopter. Having even a little wind helps ease the strain significantly, but there was little if any wind for much of the Katrina rescue period. This put additional demands on the transmission and certainly added to the stress of the pilots. But hovering was the order of the day for hoisting survivors from flooded houses below.

Several times I was on flights during which the helicopter hoisted survivors along the way to our destination. I hated to use a helicopter for travel when they were doing such important rescue work, but sometimes that was the only way to move about in the flooded city to coordinate boat rescue operations, and I always felt much better when the helicopter was hoisting while they carried me around the city. I distinctly remember looking out the side window during one flight and, in just that one direction, counting twenty-five helicopters hoisting. Others were hoisting on the other side of the helicopter as well. There were orange Coast Guard HH-65s, the larger white Coast Guard HH-60s, and the very dark National Guard and Army UH-60s, all working together, at first without an air traffic control system to manage things. That there were no collisions was a miracle in itself and a true credit to all of the pilots operating in those danger-filled skies.

But it wasn't just each other the helicopters had to avoid. There were all kinds of debris and obstacles in the wake of the storm that endangered the hoisting operations. Usually the helicopter could fly above the obstacles, but lowering the hoist cable down into the mess put the helicopter and its entire crew at risk. If the hoist cable snagged on a tree, a downed power pole, the edge of a roof, or part of a fence, the moving helicopter was now tethered to the ground. The cable could be severed in an emergency, but things don't always work as planned.

In these situations, the pilot would be flying the helicopter, holding position; the co-pilot keeping an intense eye on the other helicopters, obstacles the pilot couldn't see, and the aircraft gauges; and the crewman at the door would watch the hoist. The pilots depended on the crewman to direct the pilot as he or she maneuvered the aircraft for the best position before, during, and after the hoist. It was difficult and dangerous work, but these crews made it seem routine. No matter how easy they made it look, it must be remembered that these crews were flying with their transmissions at dangerous limits, in stifling heat, with no wind at all, surrounded by swarms of helicopters, and avoiding an endless supply of dangers to the hoist cable. These helicopter crews were both highly skilled and exceedingly brave. And that was just the men and women who stayed in the helicopter.

The rescue swimmers are in another category of brave and are highly revered in the Coast Guard. The 2006 movie *The Guardian,* starring Kevin Costner, highlighted the intense training these swimmers endure. In normal rescue operations, the rescue swimmers will jump out of the helicopter and swim to the victim struggling in the water. The swimmer will calm the person and signal for the basket or horse collar to be lowered, depending on the circumstance. The swimmer then helps the person into the basket or horse collar so that they can be hoisted up to the helicopter. Once the victim is safely onboard, the helicopter will hoist the swimmer up too then fly to drop off the rescued person. But it was different in Katrina. Typically, the swimmers would ride the cable down onto a roof and assess the situation. Often the helicopter could see one or two people from the hole in the roof, but once the swimmer reached the roof, sometimes he would find ten or twenty people huddled in the attic. Since the helicopter could only hold a few at a time, especially if it was a smaller orange HH-65, the rescue swimmers tried to make sure children were hoisted with parents to keep families together. But with very large families, that wasn't always possible. Several times frantic people tried to force their way into the rescue baskets, but the swimmers were firm and stayed in control of every situation. At least one had a gun pulled on him. He calmly said there would be no hoisting at all until things settled down and everyone followed his direction. Having total control of the helicopter tends to put things in perspective for everybody. Things calmed down and the hoists were made as planned and in an orderly manner.

Getting frantic survivors into the hoist basket could be a challenge. These people had been traumatized by the storm itself. Winds reaching 140 miles per hour had torn apart their houses and neighborhoods, ripped trees apart, and

A rescue swimmer preparing survivors for a hoist to the helicopter. (USCG)

forced deadly floodwaters into their homes. They had survived the storm by huddling in attics or on rooftops, fearing for their lives. Now a stranger offered them a tenuous means of escape: to get into and lay down flat in a little metal basket attached to a very thin-looking cable and get hoisted into the air. While in the basket, they would swing back and forth as they were lifted skyward, many likely hoping and praying that they would not be dropped. It is a frightening process, and the rescue swimmers were master talkers to convince these terrified people to give it a shot.

The helicopter crews helped out the boats too, sometimes carrying out supplies of food and water before starting their hoist operations. And sometimes they moved senior personnel around as needed to direct the operation, hoisting survivors along the way. Without a doubt there was serious heroism in the skies over New Orleans in those helicopters, and I heard many rescued people call them guardian angels.

Whatever Needed to Be Done

Rescue operations continued at a rapid pace in the city, and the Coasties were drafted into a wide range of jobs. The adventures of Gunner's Mate Second Class Oliver Haeske are pretty typical of the various tasks required during the rescue and recovery operations. Haeske was trained as a gunner's mate, meaning he was specially trained in the operation, care, and maintenance of various weapons in the Coast Guard arsenal, from 9 mm pistols, shotguns, and M16 rifles to the 25 mm and 76 mm cannons on the large cutters. In addition to his specialty training, he also earned his boat crew qualification after being assigned at Marine Safety and Security Team 91112 in New Orleans. However, like many Coasties, Haeske was soon doing jobs he never expected.

Arriving in New Orleans the day after the storm, Haeske quickly adjusted to a city in complete chaos. His first task was to help navigate the four trucks towing the four trailered 25-foot response boats to where they could be launched so they could reach the Mississippi River. This was no easy task. The 25-footers are big boats, very heavy and sometimes heavily armed with machine guns positioned fore and aft, meaning one mounted up front on the bow and one mounted on the stern on the back of the boat. These boats were designed to provide security on the water in any situation, and they are both fast and maneuverable. But on their trailers, the heavy boats were testing the limits of the trucks' ability to tow them and were proving difficult to handle on the obstructed roadways of the post-Katrina city. Trying to get these four trucks and four boats around flooded streets, downed trees, power lines, and endless debris was a slow and tedious process.

These large boats were to be deployed on the river where their size and speed could make a real difference. For use inside the city's flooded streets, they were far too big. They needed water too deep and they were too unwieldy. But once in the Mississippi River, their size, speed, and strength made them invaluable. On the river, the 25-footers and their crews did great work with the larger Coast Guard cutters *Pamlico, Clamp,* and *Greenbrier* in transporting to safety thousands of displaced refugees from the flooded city of Chalmette, located in the totally devastated St. Bernard Parish on the east bank of the river.

In addition to working on the river in the 25-footers, Haeske was involved in other operations. Along with many

Marine Safety and Security Team 91109 from San Diego, California. (USCG)

of his fellow Marine Safety and Security Team members, he provided essential security for the small FEMA flood punts. The FEMA guys were often firefighters or law enforcement officers from all over the country who answered FEMA's call for help. They came without regard for their own safety. They came because people were dying and their help was needed. They were impressive men, absolute heroes by any definition, yet often soft spoken and humble about what they were doing. After the gunfire of the first few days, when they were sometimes targeted while they were rescuing people, they were happy to have the very visible armed presence of the MSST guys like Haeske. On these missions, he was fully armed and armored and looked a lot like a SWAT team member. He not only provided the "mean and ugly" presence that seemed to provide a shield of protection around the little FEMA boats, but he was also an essential crewmember doing hands-on rescue work.

But even working within the zone of peace the MSST established around the FEMA rescue teams, these were still missions fraught with danger. Along with the more obvious and unusual hazards, like the balls of fire ants or the animals and people who had lost their grip on sanity, there were other dangers in the water that made simply driving the boat down the street a challenge at times. There were problems the boat coxswains could see, like part of a downed tree sticking up out of the water or parts of a house to be avoided. But other potential dangers lurked just under the surface. In shallow waters, most obstacles could be seen and avoided. The problem lay in deeper water where the crewmen couldn't see the obstacle through the murky depths. Here the issue was hitting the lower unit of the engine, with its spinning propeller, against a steel car, windshield, tree trunk, or other hard object. In this case, if the boat had any speed at all, the lower unit of the outboard engine would be ruined, and what had been a maneuverable rescue boat would suddenly become an unpowered raft. Mailboxes, fire hydrants, outdoor benches, tables, and even stop signs lurking just below the water all seemed to be waiting to take out an engine. This made the crews drive slowly unless they knew an area was clear and safe. It wasn't worth the risk of being stranded.

The pace of operations was brisk. These crews worked from dawn until dusk, every day. The temperature was typically in the high 90s in the days following Katrina, and a thirteen- or fourteen-hour day on the water, in the sun, without a cold drink in sight, was exhausting. And these crews did it day after day after day. The Coastie crews on the little boats usually lasted five to seven days before they were utterly drained and had to be relieved, but replacements kept flowing in and the boats kept going. Sunburn was also a real problem. These were open boats, and some volunteers from northern states got fried if they didn't use a lot of sunscreen. Most came down with the typical military ball cap, and soon the military style "boonie" hats with a full rim to protect the neck and ears from the sun became a very popular item.

Like all the FEMA and Coastie flood punt crews, the boats went house to house, often knocking on roofs or walls. The houses themselves were sometimes in bad shape, frequently structurally weakened by the serious flooding. In one case, Haeske and his FEMA crew were working in a very rough part of the city, one well known for violence before the storm. They came across a woman in the second story of a house, the ground floor being submerged. The woman was seriously overweight and it was clear that she wasn't doing well at all, but she didn't want to leave the house. Haeske tried to convince the woman to go with them in the boat, but she would not. After half an hour of talking to the woman, she finally agreed to go with the boat, but then she revealed that there were two other women in the home. Haeske was able to look through a window and saw two more seriously overweight women. It was obvious all three ladies were in rough shape and were at the point where the heat and dehydration had seriously impacted their ability to think rationally. All three were suffering from heat exhaustion, a condition where body movements are much less coordinated, the muscles are greatly weakened, and the mind is clouded. They were in trouble, yet in their misguided thinking, they felt safe in the house. It took some time and careful diplomacy, but eventually, all three ladies agreed to be evacuated in the boat.

The next problem was how to get them safely out of the house. The door on the ground floor was under water. The windows on the second floor were far too small for the ladies to crawl through and were covered by bars. Haeske took a small hatchet and, with great effort, chopped a hole in the side of the home. Once the hole was large enough for him to crawl through, he took off his body armor and weapons and squeezed into the 110-degree house. The ladies were quite upset with the new hole in their house, but they were also in serious condition and were clearly at risk of dying. Like so many in the aftermath of Katrina, they were dazed and bewildered and not thinking clearly at all. Haeske calmed the ladies, who then agreed to allow him to enlarge the hole. But now the women were afraid they would be taken to the Superdome. They had heard some ugly stories about the events and conditions at the Superdome; even in the flooded city, word traveled fast. Haeske had to convince them that they would not be taken there. By this time the National Guard had the Superdome pretty much under control, but the stories persisted for some time. Then Haeske got to work on the hole from inside the house while another crewmember worked from the outside of the house to make a hole large enough for the women to get through. Then they assisted the ladies, a daughter, mother, and grandmother, with packing up what they could and carefully helped them through the hole and down the five-foot drop into the rescue boats. The ladies were clearly dehydrated and needed first aid, which they immediately received from the crews in the boats. They were then all evacuated to safety and medical attention, but not to the Superdome.

In a similar rescue, Haeske found several dehydrated, exhausted, and angry people waiting for help. He gave them what food and water he still had and did a basic medical inspection to make sure there were no serious injuries. Then, because the people were too large to evacuate easily, he chopped an exit hole around the barred windows to get the people out of the extremely hot house. He then carefully lowered each person about seven feet into the arms of the crew in the waiting boat, and safety.

In one case, he heard faint noises coming from a flooded house. After the coxswain pushed the boat up against the roof, Haeske climbed atop the home and tore open a hole in the roof with his bare hands; his crew had not yet been supplied with tools. Obviously this took a toll on his hands, giving him cuts and lacerations, but he took no notice. Inside he found a very frail elderly man who could barely talk due to severe dehydration and hunger. He lifted the man from the house and then lowered him safely onto the waiting skiff and into the arms of emergency medical technicians.

Haeske also performed more dangerous explorations on behalf of his crew. On one mission, he entered several buildings known to harbor looters. He cleared the buildings for the rescuers who would follow him, going room by room to make sure no criminals were waiting to ambush the team. This was a very important duty with a high risk factor; it is easy to hide and ambush somebody, but finding where the ambusher is hiding can be rather difficult. Fortunately, at times the mere presence of an armed Coastie was enough to make the looters seek shelter elsewhere.

In each of these cases, Petty Officer Oliver Haeske went above and beyond to save lives. It takes a motivated man to tear a hole in a roof with his bare hands or chop a hole in the side of a house with a small hatchet to rescue people. It takes a kind man to talk with three ladies who are quite dazed, severely dehydrated, and nearing death and convince them that it is a good idea to chop a hole in their house and get them the medical attention they badly need. It takes a brave man to provide highly visible protection for his team while at the same time knowing that he is the obvious and rather easy target for any sniper in the area. It takes a dedicated man to do this day after day after day, performing hard work in tough conditions, wearing full body armor in sweltering temperatures. And it takes a generous man to give so much of himself to help others, to help those he doesn't know and will never see again. Yet while Haeske did a great job and exhibited each of these wonderful characteristics, he was but one of many out there doing the exact same thing, saving lives all over the city. The Coast Guard didn't train these young men and women to present themselves as obvious targets while providing protection for others. We didn't train them in psychology for talking to dazed and bewildered people. And we certainly didn't train them to chop holes in houses to save people in desperate need. But we did train them to do whatever needed to be done, and they did it.

I Need a Father Mulcahy!

With the intensity of the rescue operations in the city and the tremendous support we were receiving, things were going well. Commander Shannon Gilreath and his USAR team at Zephyr Field had done a superb job developing and implementing the grid system we were using, and with fully equipped boat crews heading out every morning, I felt we were doing a good job of finding and rescuing everyone there was to be found. After several days, the logistics teams had found their rhythm as well, and not only were standard supplies flowing in as fast as we could use them, but very welcome extras were found and sent to us as well. Uniform items to replace those lost or destroyed in the rescue effort were very appreciated, as were sunscreen, mosquito repellent, hand sanitizer, boonie hats, sunglasses, fresh underwear, socks, plastic bags, work gloves, hand tools, fresh coffee, body armor, and a host of other little things that made life better.

Getting these equipment and supplies out to the field was itself a major task. Petty Officer Shane Witko stepped up and kept the boats supplied. He started the operation as engineer on a 55-foot aids to navigation boat and was a key player in rescuing over 125 people stranded by the floodwaters. He also worked to evacuate more than 5,000 people from downtown New Orleans. The evacuation took a very delicate touch. These survivors were hungry, thirsty, and angry, and some were suffering mentally from the stress and shock of the hurricane, but all were safely evacuated. Witko then took on the resupply mission, and he was perfect for the job because he knew exactly what the crews in the boats needed. He dodged looters, criminal gangs, and the occasional shooter, but he kept the first responders supplied.

The exceptional work being done in these areas left me free to focus on less exciting but equally important issues. Arranging for and then managing the flood of Coasties coming to New Orleans to help was of utmost concern. Though we needed all the help we could get, every person coming down had to have a place to sleep and an assignment with a team. We had to be able to feed them, equip them with the tools they would need for the job, keep the boats fueled and running, and allow for the softer items such as showers, laundry, and portable toilet facilities. We struggled for quite a while to support the maximum number of rescue personnel, but time was critical and those needing help couldn't wait.

I also had to attend a flurry of meetings, working with the Joint Task Force the Army was setting up at Naval Air Station Joint Reserve Base Belle Chasse, visiting and supporting the Zephyr Field operation, working with city leaders, communicating with U.S. Customs, and meeting with the FEMA staff. I also had to run up to Alexandria from time to time to work complex coordination issues with the Sector staff that were sometimes best dealt with in person. With the landline phones down and cell phones not much more reliable, I spent a lot of time traveling to coordinate in person with these various groups.

One unexpected pleasure was that I had use of my office. When the looters destroyed so much of Station New Orleans, the command suite of offices and the operations center were missed. This luxury allowed me a place to stop and think, if only for a few minutes, and plan for the next event. Unfortunately even my office was not unscathed. Everything on my desk was a soggy mess from a leak in the roof. It soon because obvious that even though it had seemed important before the storm, absolutely none of the paperwork on my desk was of any relevance in our new reality. I shoved the muck into a trash bag and thus quickly and efficiently completed the pre-storm paperwork. A very welcome gift was that the bible on my desk survived, the only thing on my desk to do so. It was a bit swollen from the water but very usable, and it sits on my desk today, many years later, a quiet reminder of both the Katrina operation and God's guiding hand.

Along with ensuring that the crews received food, water, a shower, and a place to sleep, I was also very worried about the mental, emotional, and spiritual health of the men and women who were on the front lines of Katrina. These young Coasties were working very long hours, doing jobs for which they had little or no training. They were under severe emotional stress and were witnessing things no one should see. I will not go so far as to say it was like combat, but some were getting shot at, and those people I talked to who had just returned from Iraq said the stress level of this mass rescue was similar to the stress they had experienced in the

I gave a morning briefing to the crews operating out of Station New Orleans. (USCG, Mike Howell)

war. I held morning and evening meetings to pass information, give orders as needed, and to talk with the rescuers and the staff to gauge how they were doing.

Long hours weren't the problem, as most of the young Coasties could work the brutal hours we were demanding of them and still have energy left over. But the severe heat and constant exposure to the sun were wearing, and the collective strain of needing to rescue every single person out there took its toll. Being creative in solving a host of problems is fun, but it uses up mental energy. The dangers of the mission added to the stress level as well. Always having to be not only alert, but almost hyper-alert to the various dangers makes it very hard to settle down at night and very hard to sleep. Talking to crazed people, those who have been through the severe stress of the hurricane and suffering from dehydration and heat stroke while waiting for rescue, added a new level of stress. It was obvious that those long and often trying conversations to convince confused people to leave their their sauna-like homes and get into the boat was exhausting to our young men and women. And then there were the floating bodies, both animal and human, which contributed to both the horrors and the stench. In the evenings, the campers at the station would gather around a lantern that served as a "campfire" and debrief the day. They would make jokes, share what they had seen, and help each other decompress. But we clearly needed professional help. It was vital that we help these young men and women who were so bravely helping others.

Fortunately the Coast Guard Chaplain Corps sprang into action and began to send chaplains from all over the Coast Guard to work with our exhausted crews, listen to them, and minister to them. This was a gift. But I noticed we had a new chaplain every day, and this was a problem. The young Coasties needed some consistency; they needed to establish a rapport and talk to the same chaplain night after night. Building a relationship of trust was critical when we wanted them to pour their hearts out and cleanse their souls. Like many in my military generation, we all loved the *MASH* television show, and it was obvious to me that what I needed was a Father Mulcahy, a kind chaplain to talk to the crews, hear their triumphs and tragedies, listen to their stories, be their friend, hear their fears, patch them up, and get them ready to go back out again. About the time I came to this realization, I ran into an old comrade in arms. Into my office walked Lieutenant Commander Endel Lee.

Endel Lee was a Reserve Chaplain for the Eighth District, working part time for the Coast Guard. Like all Coast Guard chaplains, he was a Navy chaplain on loan to the Coast Guard and had previously served on active duty with both the Navy underway on ship and with the Marines in combat. Chaplain Lee had seen hard duty before. I first met him one night at about 2:00 AM in Mobile, Alabama, when we gathered to comfort a brand-new widow. Her husband had just killed himself over gambling debts, and our job was to gently break the bad news and help her however we could. Though the deceased wasn't one of my guys, I got the call because I was the only senior officer available in the area. Chaplain Lee got his call because he was also in the general area. We talked on the phone and met at an intersection. Then we traveled together to the lady's house. It was tough. The bikes in her front yard were the same size as the bikes in my front yard, and it really hit home, like getting kicked in the gut. Chaplain Lee and I did the best we could to comfort her, and he was amazing, even while both she and the baby in her arms cried. All we could do was provide some short-term comfort to a lady facing a very difficult and uncertain future. It was a painful night.

But once again Chaplain Lee was here just when I needed him. I explained the problem to him and told him I was keeping him. He immediately understood and was happy to stay. The head of the Chaplain Corps wasn't as pleased; it disrupted the plan. I told him to send any chaplains he wanted, but

Lee was staying at the station for the duration and the other rotating chaplains would work for him. Normally I never could have gotten away with such things, but this was a monumental crisis and I had to take care of my folks. We also had work-life counselors working with us, civilians in the Coast Guard with training in crisis counseling. I asked them to work with Chaplain Lee as well; he was my go-to guy for these matters. Chaplain Lee did an amazing job, as I knew he would. He went from campfire to campfire every night, talking to the young men and women, debriefing them, counseling them, telling a joke or two, comforting them. He did quite a lot to keep these fine young Coasties sane, fully operational, and raring to go. He helped them get a good night's sleep so they would be fresh each and every morning, at the crack of dawn. I can't say enough about his exceptional performance. I saw him help confused, exhausted, and sometimes highly emotional people, and within a short time he would help them regroup, refocus, and repair themselves so that they could sleep soundly.

He was also worried about me, as I was running pretty hard. He knew I was a Christian and wanted to get me to a church service, which we were holding every night in the center courtyard of the upper deck of the building. But my schedule was such that I wasn't free when they were taking place. These were general Christian services, open to everybody and arranged so anybody would feel comfortable in any service. Finally I had a free moment and Chaplain Lee grabbed me and took me to the courtyard, where we enjoyed a Catholic mass. He laughed and said, "This is pretty funny: two Baptists here in a Catholic mass!" And I was refreshed, just as he knew I would be. In times like this, I don't think it really matters which flavor Christian you are. The Lord honors us because we were honoring him.

It is also important to note that the military chaplains were not trying to evangelize; they are trained to minister to anyone of any denomination or faith, or no faith at all. They

Chaplain Endel Lee knew exactly what the young men and women needed after a tough day rescuing people and witnessing the horrors of the aftermath of Katrina. His combat experience in Iraq was very much appreciated. He was one of my personal heroes. (USCG, Mike Howell)

stayed within their mandate and did a fine job. But as the old military saying goes, "There are no atheists in foxholes." During times of great crisis people tend to seek the Lord, and I noticed this during Katrina as well. Many of the people I was working with felt a strong sense of being part of a great effort, working toward a higher purpose, of doing God's work. Everybody involved with the Katrina rescue operation was changed in some way. Personally, I found a closer relationship to the Lord. Normally I am a pretty self-sufficient guy, as all Coasties are trained to be, but for the first time in my life I had to absolutely depend on the Lord, and he came through for me. It was a life-changing experience. And to be sure, I was not the only one who came away a changed person.

The Rescues Continue

There were some rescues that were easier than others, and some that will stay with the rescuers forever. Fear and often absolute terror permeated the flooded streets, and in many respects, the entire city. Many of those in the flooded areas, particularly those in the housing projects, could not swim. Some of these people were truly panicked at the thought of falling into the water, and our flood punts looked uncomfortably small to people who were already scared by the rising water in their homes. They also knew the waters were getting more polluted by the day, which increased their concerns of not only falling in but also simply getting splashed. The frequent gunfire was also troubling to both the rescuers and those the Coast Guard crews were rescuing. Often they felt safe in their homes but had serious reservations about getting into an orange boat that could be an easy target. These fears and concerns frequently made it very hard to convince stranded and even injured people to get into a boat so they could be evacuated to a safe place.

On the other hand, these distressed people were often out of food, didn't have clean water, had wounds that needed first aid, lacked bathroom facilities, and were slowly dying from the extreme heat inside their homes. It's not obvious until the power goes out, but many modern buildings don't have the large windows, high ceilings, and even French doors that made houses reasonably comfortable in the typical sweltering New Orleans summer before air-conditioning was invented. These modern buildings become heat boxes, and humans get heat soaked. If the body can't cool down at night after soaking up 115-degree temperatures all day, that person will be mentally compromised. They can die of dehydration or heat stroke and not even realize they are in danger.

Presenting a different challenge were those who were too eager to be rescued. The flood punts were small 16-foot flatboats, and people jumping into them too fast could destabilize and capsize them. If the weight inside the boat is distributed unevenly, they tip, then everybody gets wet, or worse. Another problem was posed by those people demanding to get rescued first, particularly healthy, able-bodied men who, in the tradition of maritime rescues, should have had the manners and good sense to let the women and children go first. Our policy was to rescue those most at risk first, then come back for everybody else on the next round. It was very encouraging to all of us to occasionally find those

Coast Guard and police officers working together in a Coastie boat. (USCG, PA1 Bauer)

DART team members launching the boats, with a PSU Coastie for security. (USCG, PA1 Bauer)

powerful men in the population who helped keep order and ensured that the elderly, sickly, or injured as well as the women and children went first. These men greatly assisted the rescue operation.

On that first day, when the water was still rising, Boatswain's Mate First Class Eric Gonzalez and Marine Science Technician Second Class Richard Forte were working at the frantic pace required of every Coastie in the city. With two firefighters assisting in the flood punt, they saved more than sixty-five people and took them back to the makeshift launch point. Their most dramatic rescue occurred as Gonzalez and Forte approached a heavily damaged two-story house with two victims signaling for help on the second story. Unable to approach from the front of the house due to a fence, a submerged car, a downed tree, and downed power lines, Gonzalez searched for a different way to reach the two survivors. Carefully, they used boat hooks to lift the power lines while the boat went under them. They then shut off the engine and used boat hooks to position the boat in the driveway between the houses, with very little room on either side. The first individual out was a young man in his late teens or early twenties, and he was able to make the eight-foot drop from the windowsill to the boat. Unfortunately as he fell into the boat, he knocked one of the firefighters overboard into the water. At the same time the young man's heavyset grandmother climbed out onto the windowsill, and the windowsill began to crack. The crew members worked as a team to quickly grab the firefighter and pull him back aboard as they also maneuvered the boat to place it under the grandmother. As they were getting the firefighter back onboard, the windowsill broke, dumping the grandmother. Just in time they turned to catch the grandmother, keeping her from falling overboard. They safely transported both the grandmother and her grandson safely back to the launch site, then turned around and got underway again to save more lives.

Boatswain's Mate Second Class Kevin Biami was serving as the boat crewman on a flood punt in a heavily flooded housing project. His team was responsible for rescuing almost five hundred people from these housing complexes and air-lifting several hundred more. He was involved in two great stories that day. The first occurred when his crew encountered a young woman in her early twenties who was nine months pregnant. Treading water, she was physically exhausted. It also appeared that she was in labor and was clearly delirious as a result of her ordeal. In her delirium, she was afraid of the boat and seem scared to even get out of the water, even though she appeared to be close to drowning. She was too weak to help herself over the side of the boat and she was too slippery and heavy for Biami to pull her over the side. Instead Biami coached her gently, forcing her to think

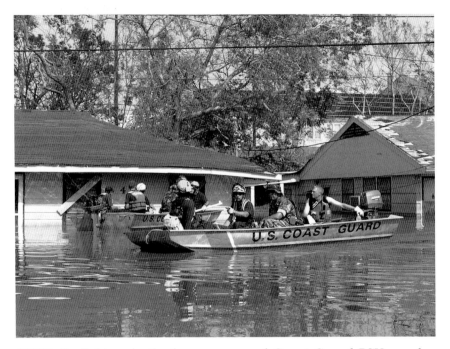

FEMA firefighters in the bow, an armed Coast Guard PSU member amidships for security, and a Coastie driving the boat. The sun was brutal, as the temperatures were usually in the mid- to high 90s every day, and as expected, the humidity was oppressive. (USCG, PA1 Bauer)

of the baby and not to give up. They were able to tow her over to the top of a nearby flooded car. Using the flooded car as a ramp, she managed to pull herself up level with the boat, but she couldn't stand or sit up. The only way to get her into the boat was to slowly roll her over the side and into the small flood punt. Once in the boat, her water broke, and she went into active labor. Overloaded, the boat sat very low in the water with almost no freeboard to spare, meaning it was loaded so heavily that water was lapping at the edge of the boat and it was in serious danger of sinking. Biami and his coxswain had to get the woman back to the landing and medical attention as quickly as possible so that she could be safely delivered of her child, but because the boat was overloaded they were forced to drive slowly through the floodwaters. The situation required finesse as they maneuvered the boat. Once they reached the landing, they carefully helped the young woman out of the boat and arranged an air lift for her to ensure she and her unborn child received proper medical attention.

In the second case, Biami and his crew were working the same housing project, which contained literally hundreds of flood victims begging, yelling, and demanding help from the second and third stories of the complexes, more people than they could help at one time. As a boatswain's mate, Kevin Biami was trained to drive boats and rescue people in terrible conditions, racing through the crashing waves on the open ocean. When ships were sinking or people were in serious trouble, Coasties like Kevin Biami would get the call. But this was a very different world from what he was trained for, and he quickly adapted to the situation. Biami was forced to triage the rescues based on the most pressing needs, trying to take the injured or those with medical problems first. Many of the stranded people were scared or even terrified; many of them were hungry and thirsty; and all of them were very hot and miserable. As might be expected, everybody wanted to go first, and not being able to go first caused some people to lash out in anger.

In this deteriorating situation, Biami was directed to find a certain elderly man, a Mr. Johnson, who was confined to a wheelchair and had a feeding tube inserted in his abdomen. Mr. Johnson was out of food and not doing well. Though a trained law enforcement officer, Biami didn't have a weapon or body armor; those things would come later in the operation. The only way to find Mr. Johnson was to go into the building and look for him while his crew member stayed with the boat. Though unarmed and hugely outnumbered by some pretty hostile people, Petty Officer Biami jumped out of the boat and onto the porch of the housing complex. Only after jumping over the side did he discover the actual depth of the water was about four and half feet deep and came within an inch of topping his chest waders, the only protection he had from the putrid water. Once inside the building he went up the darkened stairs to the second floor searching for Mr. Johnson. Other people within the building and across the street began yelling, demanding that he take them instead. It appeared likely a riot would break out over his attempt to rescue Mr. Johnson.

Biami found an extremely large and powerful-looking man and recruited his help in not only finding Mr. Johnson but also keeping some order in the building so the elderly gentleman could be saved. This brave man, whose name is lost to history, succeeded in both finding Mr. Johnson and restoring order. Mr. Johnson was indeed in a wheelchair and out of food, but he and his wife were deathly afraid of the water and didn't want to leave. Biami convinced them they had to leave; the older gentlemen obviously needed medical attention rather urgently. With the help of his new partner, Biami carried Mr. Johnson in the wheelchair back down the stairs, lifted him over his head to keep him out of the filthy water, which likely would have killed him if it had come into contact with the feeding tube. Then they placed him in the boat. Mr. Johnson's wife was also in pretty rough shape, so they put her in a chair and carried her down to the boat as well. Finally, Biami climbed back into the boat himself, and after the boat returned to the makeshift landing, he arranged an airlift for Mr. Johnson and his wife. Then, in the way of the dozens of boat crews and hundreds of Coast Guard men and women throughout the flooded city and its surrounding communities, they set out again to save lives.

Relief and Recovery

The Coast Guard operation was an amazing thing to participate in. We never expected to run such a major rescue operation inside a city; it was beyond anything we could have possibly envisioned. But it worked because the Coast Guard is small and adaptable. A common inside joke is that we have to be "*Semper* Gumby," a word play on our official motto, "*Semper Paratus,*" which means "Always Ready." Thus the joke is that we must be always flexible.

Aside from our flexibility, the Coast Guard rescue mission worked because it had to work. There was no one else available to do the job. Local New Orleans agencies were quickly overwhelmed and were often victims themselves. The police and fire departments were seriously degraded by the flooding and destruction, and many officers were trapped in their own homes, victims of the flood themselves. State agencies like the Louisiana Department of Wildlife and Fisheries and the Louisiana State Police did amazing work, but they weren't big enough for a rescue operation of the magnitude Katrina required. The Louisiana National Guard provided invaluable help in various parts of the city, showing their tenacity and resilience, but their local headquarters and much of their equipment were completely submerged in the massively flooded 9th Ward. As the rescue operation progressed, more and more National Guard troops would make their welcome presence known in many areas of the city.

At the national level, the Department of Defense was hamstrung by politics and the laws on the books at that time. The armed forces were not able to deploy into Louisiana for

We threw the safety rules out the window to get the job done. Using a ladder placed in a small boat to access a building was crazy . . . (USCG)

operations until Governor Kathleen Blanco requested their assistance from the president, but she did not make this request for over a week. This meant that the Army, Navy, Marines, and Air Force were on hot standby. Having worked in the Pentagon on a previous assignment with the Navy and having served in NATO headquarters in Italy, at a joint command in California, and aboard a Navy guided missile cruiser, I knew very well the tremendous capability that the Department of Defense can bring to bear on a problem. However, as with any large organization, there is some lead and preparation time. In this case that lead time was minimized as the armed forces prepared themselves while waiting for the authorization to deploy. Once Governor Kathleen Blanco requested assistance, things happened quickly. Joint Task Force Katrina had been established at the Naval Air Station Joint Reserve Base in Belle Chasse,

. . . And yet very effective. It was truly a miracle that no one was injured, none of the 33,500 people we rescued nor the hundreds of Coasties performing the rescues. Given our extreme operating environment and what we had to do to rescue all these people in the shortest amount of time possible, it became obvious that the Lord was with us. (USCG)

where the helicopters were operating. The First Cavalry of the Army arrived, along with the Marines, the Navy, the Air Force, and more National Guard troops from states across the nation. Eventually more than twenty-seven thousand military personnel would deploy to help in the storm-ravaged city.

We worked closely with the Army's 82nd Airborne Division in the joint FEMA and Coast Guard operation based out of Zephyr Field. The 82nd Airborne is an amazingly powerful force, made for getting into a nasty situation quickly and defeating every enemy in sight. The 82nd started arriving at Zephyr Field on September 7, which was Day Nine of the rescue, and began assisting with rescues almost immediately.

These Airborne Rangers integrated smoothly into the Coast Guard operation, with the Rangers providing security in the flood punts, much as the Coastie MSST and PSU teams were doing. Major General William Caldwell, the commander of the 82nd Airborne Division, provided excellent support to the Coasties and commented that he was impressed with the Coast Guard operation. The general assigned his inspector general, Lieutenant Colonel Dyer, as his liaison to the Unified Command at Zephyr Field. The 82nd brought full helicopter support, which made operations that much more effective. By Day Ten the water level was going down steadily, and the 82nd Airborne began using their high-water trucks in some areas, relieving the boats that could no longer navigate the increasingly shallow waters. As directed by General Russell Honoré, the commanding general of the entire Department of Defense operation in Joint Task Force Katrina, the 82nd supported the Coast Guard where the boats were running and the Coasties supported the 82nd where the trucks could take the lead. The 82nd Airborne also took charge of the body recovery, a very delicate and difficult task.

As the water level continued to drop, some agencies began withdrawing their boats. Their teams were worn out. Yet the Coast Guard continued to send boat crews and new flood punts into New Orleans to fill the gaps and finish the comprehensive search of the city. At the peak of our operation, we had more than sixty Coast Guard flood punts working out of Zephyr Field. Each area of the city was searched three times by boat. The hasty search was first, a rapid search and rescue where call-outs were made and anyone who responded was rescued. Once the entire city was searched in this manner, the primary search started. Rescuers carefully went from house to house, physically touching each building, knocking on walls or roofs, looking for survivors. Once the primary search had been completed in all flooded areas, the secondary search commenced. Once again teams went house by house and room by room to ensure none were missed. These searches continued until all rescue operations came to a stop as the teams evacuated in anticipation of Hurricane Rita. Fortunately the searches were almost complete by September 19, when preparations for the next storm began.

Like Katrina just three weeks earlier, Hurricane Rita was a Category 5 storm as it approached the Louisiana coast. Thankfully for New Orleans, Rita made landfall much farther to the west on September 24. Rita became even more powerful than Katrina while the storm was over the Gulf of Mexico, but, like Katrina, Rita lost some of its strength before making landfall. However, as with Katrina, the storm surge was still very powerful and quite destructive. Although the city saw some minor flooding as a result of the storm, Rita caused tremendous damage out on the bayou. The bayou area is a patchwork of land and water covering the southernmost parts of Louisiana and populated by a strong and independent people very much at home on the water. While most of these people evacuated, some stayed behind and were caught by Rita's powerful surge. As with Katrina the month before, the water rushed in and just kept coming, building higher and higher as it washed away everything in its path. The destruction was immense in those areas hit by the storm surge. Even though the people there are used to hurricanes and have their homes built up on stilts, this storm surge of water was far beyond what a regular hurricane would produce.

The little Coast Guard flood punts did not play a leading role in the Rita rescues, as there were numerous boats already in the bayou areas that were well suited to that task. However, the Coast Guard helicopters were critical to rescue operations right after the storm thundered through. In this case, the rescues were spread out over a larger area and the helicopters needed direction to find those in desperate conditions. Fortunately, Boatswain's Mate First Class Karyn Boxwell was positioned in low-lying Terrebonne Parish and ready for the job.

Boxwell was the Executive Petty Officer at Aids to Navigation Team Dulac, a very small Coast Guard base way out on the bayou. Driving there the first time, I was struck by the mobile homes up on stilts, often ten feet or more in the air. Boxwell was the second in command at the ANT, as the Aids to Navigation Teams are called. The team had evacuated, just as they had for Katrina the month before. In the rush to get the 55-foot boat out and all the equipment at the base either evacuated or moved to safety, the computer was left behind. Boxwell was sent back to Dulac to retrieve the computer, a piece of equipment important to the operation of the team. On her way back out of the base the storm hit and she took refuge in a local fire station. The water rushed in from the storm surge, and she found herself on the roof of the fire station. Trapped on the roof, she called me, asking what to do next.

I was back at Station New Orleans. We had evacuated the entire trailer park that we had accumulated around the station; several hundred Coasties packed up their gear and departed smoothly yet quickly. It was surreal to watch the tents taken down, the trailers hooked up to trucks, and the entire operation head out of the now empty compound, a long line of RVs and campers, all heading north to safety across the Causeway Bridge. There were three or four of us who had stayed behind as a bare-bones watch. When it became obvious that Rita was heading west of New Orleans, we all breathed a sigh of relief. We had feared the levees would break again and flood the city once more. The breached levees in and around New Orleans had all been repaired, but the repairs were temporary at best and the levees could not have weathered another major storm. But now we faced a new problem.

We knew there would be people in serious trouble, people needing rescue out on the bayou farther west, and for the Coast Guard, that meant mostly helicopter rescues. Talking to the helicopter crews, it became obvious they needed a forward air controller, someone on the ground in the flooded area to direct them to people needing rescue. Then I got the call from Karyn Boxwell. Her presence was yet another miracle and saved many lives. Boxwell should have been far away, safely evacuated with the rest of the ANT. Yet there she was, in exactly the right place at exactly the right time. She was a seasoned veteran to different types of Coast Guard operations, and she made excellent decisions, relaying information from local firefighters regarding the whereabouts of those needing rescue and directing the Coast Guard helicopters. Though she was trained as a boat driver, she quickly adapted to the new mission and many people were rescued as a result.

After the limited Rita rescue operation, our focus shifted as we began to put our Coast Guard stations and facilities back together and care for our own people. Though many of our stations were destroyed and would remain inoperable for many months, taking care of our people was by far the more important task. Unlike many civilians who lived in the city and could relocate until conditions improved and their jobs returned, the Coasties were assigned to work here and had to stay.

While working conditions were bad enough, living conditions were even worse for many. The Coast Guard first provided trailers and RVs and later portable buildings to serve as office spaces for those units destroyed or severely damaged, but many of our people were living in hotels, their houses uninhabitable after the floodwaters of Katrina. Even houses in Metairie that only had a foot of flooding were rendered completely unusable, along with everything in them, because mold quickly took over the entire house and its contents in the heat. The homes had to be gutted then sprayed with mold killer and left to dry before the interior of the house could be rebuilt.

For many of our families, after a couple of months of living in a hotel, they were provided with a FEMA trailer, a very basic camper to live in. Some said it was better than being in a hotel because it could be put on their own property while they worked on their house. Some said it was worse than the hotel, as the living space was much smaller. But in any case, we had a lot of Coasties living in FEMA trailers for a very long time. One couple, a pair of married officers with five children, was issued a FEMA trailer and then bought an RV. The husband slept in one with the boys and the wife slept in the other with the girls. I can only imagine the unbelievable stress this created for the family. It was nearly two years before they could move back into their house.

This timeline for recovery was not unusual. It was unbelievably hard for families trying to rebuild. With hundreds of thousands of homes damaged or destroyed across six parishes, an invasion of insurance adjusters descended on New Orleans, with precious few contractors or building supplies available to put everything right. A family might manage to gut their home, reducing it to studs and a roof, but drywall was impossible to find. Compounding the tragedy was that when building supply stores did manage to stock the coveted drywall, much of it was Chinese drywall that made people very sick with toxic fumes. Many homes had to be gutted yet again. Just finding someone to install drywall was a challenge that could take months. And you would first have to find an electrician and a plumber to rewire and check the damaged circuitry and plumbing, processes that after Katrina often took several months themselves. Not only that, many homeowners had to fight for their insurance benefits, as some companies were claiming that houses weren't covered because the flood damage wasn't hurricane related.

The stresses and strains on our Coast Guard families were enormous, but they responded superbly while they put their Coast Guard world back together, often making it better than it was before the storm. As proof of their efforts, in the years following Katrina, numerous New Orleans units received the Sumner I. Kimball Readiness Award. The Kimball award is given to small boat units such as small boat stations, aids to navigation teams, and the occasional marine safety unit that operates a small boat. Each of these units is subject to a very rigorous inspection of both equipment and personnel. These inspections are highly competitive, requiring months of preparation and training in every possible aspect of boat operations. With the 41-foot boats being thirty and forty years old and the 55-footers being even older, maintaining them in states of perfect readiness while still operating them was tough. For the personnel, making sure everybody had proper training records when many computer files were lost in the floodwaters of Katrina was a challenge. Typically only the top five percent of the boat units in the Coast Guard earn the Kimball award. But the Coasties in and around New Orleans responded with amazing results. In 2007 and 2008, Sector New Orleans units earned twenty-five percent of the Kimball awards presented nationwide. This was an

Semper Paratus. (USCG)

astounding achievement, especially since most of these units operated out of trailers for a year or two after the storm.

I was so very blessed to have not only witnessed but been a part of the recovery and rebirth of New Orleans. At that time I had twenty-three years as a commissioned officer in the Coast Guard, and had I not been assigned to New Orleans during Katrina, I would have been desperately trying to get to New Orleans after the storm, as was the case with so many Coasties. I saw some of the worst in human behavior after the storm, and I worked with some of the finest people I have ever known. The Coast Guard did many amazing things, and I saw the hand of God in many more. Roughly 33,000 people were rescued by the Coast Guard in Katrina, about 25,000 of them by boat. Through it all, none of these people or our Coasties were injured during the rescue, in itself a miracle of significant proportions. We had to stretch and bend the rules to fit the circumstances. We ran our men and women until they were exhausted. We loaded the boats with more than they could officially hold. And we had exactly the right people at the right place at the right time, before the storm, during the storm, and after the storm, over and over and over again. And I learned that if you call on him, the Lord will be there to get you through any disaster. He takes care of his people, even in the worst of circumstances. Like so many people prayed when the Coasties showed up to rescue them as they waited helplessly, "Thank you, Lord!"

Index